THE BETTER LIFE BOOK

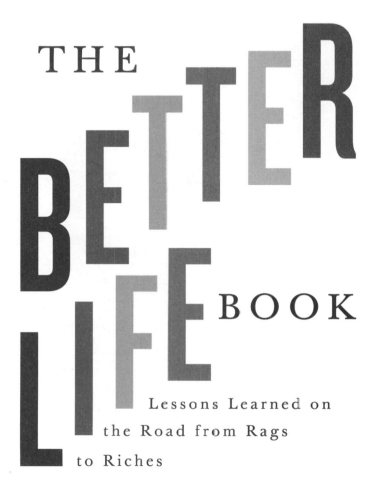

THE BETTER LIFE BOOK

Lessons Learned on the Road from Rags to Riches

ROSEMARIE FRANCIS

LIFETREE MEDIA

Published by
LifeTree Media Ltd.
www.lifetreemedia.com

Distributed by
Greystone Books Ltd.
www.greystonebooks.com

Cataloguing data available from Library and Archives Canada
ISBN 978-0-9936530-4-9 (hardcover)
ISBN 978-0-9936530-5-6 (epub)
ISBN 978-0-9936530-9-4 (pdf)

Editing by Maggie Langrick
Copyediting by Carol Volkart
Cover design by David Drummond
Interior design by Ingrid Paulson
Printed and bound in Canada by Friesens

For my mom and dad,
Roy and Leonie Smith,
who lived through their
own personal challenges.

For my daughters,
who every day help me see the joy
in the smallest of gestures and who
remind me of the innocence of each child
and the potential within.

For my dear friends and family members,
Carey, Areta, Shelly, Judith
and Patricia, whose support has
been unwavering.

CONTENTS

Introduction / 1

LESSON ONE:
Be Your Own Believer / 7

LESSON TWO:
Create Your Future From The Future / 31

LESSON THREE:
Map Out Your Plan / 47

LESSON FOUR:
Build a Network Of Supporters / 65

LESSON FIVE:
Set Yourself Up For Success / 85

LESSON SIX:
Make You Your Top Priority / 107

LESSON SEVEN:
Magnify Your Existence / 131

Acknowledgments / 149

*My brother, mother
and myself in Garson,
Manitoba, circa 1975.
Even as a child,
I knew there was
a better life out
there for me.*

INTRODUCTION

*"Any fact facing us is not as important
as our attitude toward it,
for that determines our success or failure."*

NORMAN VINCENT PEALE

Everyone has a story to tell or a journey to share. Mine is extraordinary, and over the years, many of my friends and acquaintances have urged me to share it with the world. I'm doing so now not to show off, gain notoriety or make money but because I've learned valuable lessons on my amazing journey that I hope will inspire others who are seeking to build their own successful lives.

As my book details, my life began in poverty and deprivation, in family circumstances bordering on neglect. By the time I was 18, I'd achieved my dream of moving to the city, begun my education as a Certified Management Accountant, and purchased the first of a long sequence of properties I would buy and sell over the years. I achieved my CMA designation by age 21, went into sales and marketing, and by the time I was 24, was earning over $100,000 a year. I've founded and run companies, entered the world of philanthropy and now in my 40s, I'm raising my family on a beautiful waterfront property on the West Coast.

None of this came without a lot of learning, and it's those lessons I'm now passing along to you. Some are down-to-earth practical — drink water if your tight budget won't extend to wine! — but many are about the psychological growth and self-care that are an essential part of achieving success. Believing in myself and taking care of myself were key to my journey, just as your own self-confidence and self-knowledge will be essential to yours.

I had setbacks, challenges and even some regrets, but they provided some of my best learning experiences, and I hope those lessons will help you too.

As a person who set out very early in life to overcome my disadvantages and rise in the world, I would have loved a book like this to guide my journey, tell me I was not alone, and more importantly, show me that there was a way out. I figured out many of my strategies on my own, but nobody lives in a bubble, and I was fortunate to meet many inspiring guides, sponsors and mentors along the way.

They include Peter Thomas and Vince Poscente, both gifted authors and motivational speakers in their own right, who have inspired me to tell my story.

Each day when I look at my own three daughters, I recall my own childhood and realize once again how blessed my children are to have been born into a family with education and means. But I know there are many others growing up without their advantages, and I believe we need a community conversation about the impact of poverty and bullying on children and how to tackle it. In the meantime, I hope this book will provide some inspiration to parents seeking a way out of poverty, as well as to people simply searching for a better life for themselves.

We learn from each other by sharing our stories, and this is my contribution to that communal conversation.

BE YOUR OWN BELIEVER

*"The most common way people give up
their power is by thinking they don't have any."*

ALICE WALKER

Augustl, 1984

The two green garbage bags in the back of my 1972 yellow Comet contained ten shirts, both long and short sleeved, including my favorite one of royal blue with Elizabethan sleeves and a Peter Pan collar; one pair of Lee Jeans and four pairs of pants, stained from my waitressing shifts at the local greasy spoon; four pairs of full-coverage underwear, stretched out with holes along the seams (my mom always said, "Nobody sees them anyway, so who cares what they look like?"); three bras, faded from years of laundering; one pair of cheap runners; two pairs of low-heeled cheap dress shoes, one white and one black; two dresses; one pair of purple corduroy pedal pushers with a pair of black suspenders; a white-trimmed turquoise string bikini; one baby-blue winter coat with dirt-stained sleeves; four pairs of white exercise socks with holes in the toes; one pair of blue nylon lace-up winter boots; some old high school textbooks; a blanket from my mom; a small box of tampons; a makeup bag that held my mascara, purple and white eye shadow, pink lipstick and other cosmetics; one bottle each of Flex shampoo and conditioner; a curling iron, hair brush and hair dryer.

It was all I owned in the world. And as meager as it may seem now, to 17-year-old me, it represented an achievement that symbolized not only where I had come from, but where I was going.

My sights were set far, far away from the cramped and cluttered three-room shack in which I was raised on the outskirts of Garson, Manitoba. That shack's windows were held together by the magic of duct tape and plastic. The luxury of indoor plumbing was for other, richer folks. We got by with a "slop" pail for kitchen wastewater and an "it" pail, a five-gallon bucket, for our human waste. Even in the excruciating cold of a Prairie winter, my mother had the job of hauling both pails outside for dumping every other day. Our only source of heat was a dark brown metal oil burner in what we called our living room. The house got awfully cold when the outside temperature would drop to −40 Celsius. At night, I would lie in bed scraping ice off the walls to which my sheets were often frozen stuck.

I shared that bedroom with my entire family: my mother, my father and my older brother, whose mission in life was to make me his personal verbal and physical punching bag.

I view my family members with compassion now, and I understand each had their problems, but they were a dysfunctional bunch who unwittingly helped propel me out of that little household as fast as I could go.

Even as a child, I could see how my father's insecurities poisoned his life. I never truly knew the source of his demons, but I suspect he blamed himself for his alcoholic father walking out on his family when my dad was just a boy. Fatherless, he got into a lot of trouble with the law. Worse, even though he was smart and could have gone further, he dropped out of school after the eighth grade because he thought it wasn't important. That mistake haunted him for the rest of his life; I'd see it whenever he was around educated people. He'd turn emotional and argumentative, like he thought he had something to prove but always felt he came up short.

As a young man, he got a job selling men's clothes and then spices, and later became a welder with a farm machinery company. But in a working man's community dotted with mills and limestone quarries, the pinnacle of success was a union job. When my father got into the Teamsters Union, with its glorious promise of job security and a pension plan, his conversation turned endlessly to the golden day of his retirement. Then he'd finally enjoy his life...

Meanwhile, his dissatisfaction and unhappiness found its outlets, poking out in many destructive ways. He had affairs. In my early years, he drank. He'd often disappear for entire weekends, reappearing only to take his anger out on my mother with his fists. When I was a teenager, he replaced alcohol with addictions to pain medication and sleeping pills. He suffered from depression and other psychological issues. Although he never set foot in a church, he became obsessed with religion and theories about the end of the world. Armageddon and World War III became staples of conversation in our home, and he was obsessed with hoarding what little money we had. By the time I was in high school, we could have afforded a nicer house with indoor plumbing, but the "slop" and "it" pails remained part of our lives as he chose to keep his family in impoverished living conditions. As the years passed, our dilapidated shack fell into more and more disgraceful disrepair.

Even worse than his addictions and obsessions was his verbal and mental abuse of his family. All of us were targets; we were all stupid and not good enough.

My mother and brother, both mentally challenged, bore the brunt of his anger. My mother, who I later discovered had an IQ of 78, could barely read. My brother had a learning disability. He had trouble grasping basic concepts and often got confused when reading or doing simple math problems. Other kids teased and bullied him, and he had trouble forming friendships or even just getting along with people. He couldn't look people in the eye when he talked to them. To this day, he still struggles with the basics of life.

As for my mother, she was trapped, especially when my brother and I were very young. Unable to learn to drive, she was stuck in that isolated shack caring for us on her own while her husband ran around drinking and having affairs. When the snow came, she was the one who shoveled the driveway as well as the pathways to the outhouse and to the neighbor's water pump, where we got our water in five-gallon pails.

After a while, she seemed to just give up. She didn't try to improve her reading skills. She didn't care what she looked like. She spent hours in front of the TV every day, living her life through the characters in the soap operas. While she did work for a while as a house cleaner, and later at a chicken-processing plant, I have many memories of her just sitting at the table staring into space, with a catatonic look on her face. It was as though she had checked out of life because if she acknowledged the pain unfolding around her, it might have been too much to bear.

Between my father's angry unhappiness and my mother's passive defeat, I wanted out of there as soon as possible. But I wasn't getting out just so I could replicate their sad lives in my own way. My plan was to have a different kind of life altogether.

To that end, I'd been preparing my escape since I was very young. Learning. Earning. Planning.

By the time I graduated from high school and was stuffing those green garbage bags into my car, I was well on the way to putting my plans into execution. I'd already proven I could take care of myself, buying all my own clothes and toiletries throughout high school with money earned from my waitressing job. That job — endless rounds of dishing out hamburgers, milkshakes and coffees at the local greasy spoon — had paid for everything I was taking with me, and even the $600 car I was taking it away in. But the most important thing I was carrying with me that day was my belief in myself.

That self-belief has been the foundation of my entire life, and has made all the difference in getting me to where I am today.

Most tales about people in dire circumstances include a white knight, or at least an outsider who gives the struggling hero (or heroine) a boost. Such people are magic and I've been lucky to have several in my life, but the first and most pivotal for me came in the form of a kind elderly neighbor.

Mrs. Mary Chromiak ran a vegetable stand in front of her home, selling produce from her garden. As a curious child, I would often spend time with her, watching her with the customers, eager to get involved. She let me help bag up the produce and keep the stand in order, and I thrived on the sense of usefulness these small responsibilities gave me. Over time she gradually gave me more and more to do. By the age of nine, I was able to take on the entire responsibility of serving customers and taking their payments. I took these tasks very seriously, counting the money carefully and feeling very proud of my grown-up role. Sometimes Mrs. Chromiak would let me keep a little bit of the money for myself, an unbelievable privilege for which I was very grateful.

It was my first taste of the world that would become my life — handling money, selling, dealing with customers. But more importantly, it taught me I could do something; I was good at something. It was the beginning of believing in myself.

Over the years that followed, my confidence would sometimes shatter. Many times I doubted myself so much I would get scared and shut down, beating myself up for what I saw as my failings. But when I first left home, all I knew for sure was that failure wasn't an option — I had to be successful. I believed that I could get a job and an apartment, and that was enough to get going with. Even those small victories were head and shoulders above what I was leaving behind.

Three decades later, with a successful career in sales and marketing behind me, I have financial security, substantial real estate holdings, and I am raising three lovely daughters in a beautiful waterfront home on the West Coast. I have expensive cars, stylish clothes and my home has not one but seven bedrooms, along with seven bathrooms.

From this vantage point, I can tell you that your belief in yourself is the foundation upon which everything good is built. Every positive contribution you make to the world around you, every beautiful creation, every act of courage or love springs from this self-belief that says: "I am worthy of doing, having and creating great things." Despite my upbringing, I have created a life in which I have, do and create those wonderful things.

To complete the circle, I now want to share with others what I have learned along the way. And so, my advice begins at the very first step on this journey: before you can set goals or take any action toward them, you absolutely must believe in yourself.

If you doubt yourself or put yourself down, you'll subconsciously walk yourself right into a life of discontentment and frustration. You'll wonder why others have all the luck. You'll be filled with regret for not doing the things you wanted when you had the chance. You'll blame your circumstances and feel powerless to make a change.

Moving from self-doubt to self-belief is easier said than done. If you're honestly feeling insecure or down in the dumps, you can't change that as easily as flipping a switch. But I've worked on this issue for my entire life, and I have found that with effort and the right intentions, it can be done.

✺ STIFLE YOUR NEGATIVE INNER VOICE

The very first step is to be aware of the conversation in your head. Although that voice is private and internal, its influence is far-reaching. Thoughts of being "not good enough" or that "somebody else deserves this more" will bring your creativity and inspiration to a grinding halt.

This negative voice visits all of us at some point, often playing in the background of our minds where it remains unchallenged. It's often worse when we take a risk or try something new. "This is never going to work," it says as we put ourselves out there in a new and scary way. "I'll never pull this off; I'm not good enough or smart enough."

I noticed, even when I was very young, that negative self-talk was accompanied by some definite physical sensations. Whenever I was in the presence of anyone I considered important or authoritative (almost any adult), I would shut down. I would avoid speaking or making eye contact, feeling I had nothing interesting to say and that if they looked into my eyes, they would see that I was really a worthless person. These thoughts were often accompanied by a tightness in my stomach and chest, and a knot in my throat. My body would feel ill at ease, my forehead would furrow, and I would freeze.

The problem continued into my young adulthood as I was exposed to more and more successful people. I'd still break into a cold sweat, clam up and feel all those other uncomfortable physical sensations.

My body was telling me I shouldn't be having this conversation in my head. It was saying loud and clear, "I don't like what I'm hearing. Can you please stop it?" Each of us has this ability to tune into our body wisdom. The key is to pay attention and stop the negative self-talk in its tracks.

When you find your mind heading in this direction, take note of the sensations in your body. How do you feel? Is there a tightness in your chest or in your stomach? Do you feel fatigued? Are you sweating or starting to feel clammy? This is your body's way of telling you it doesn't like what it's hearing and to please stop.

Where do our negative internal conversations come from? At some point we heard hurtful messages like "you're stupid" or "you're a loser." Repeated often enough, these taunts wormed themselves inside us, and at some point, we decided they were the truth. Unless we challenge these beliefs, they will lead to insecurity, inner turmoil and impede our chances of living life to its full potential.

My peers had many things to tease me about, but one of the main ones was my disgraceful home. Their taunting became worse in the fall and winter, when the trees lost their foliage, removing the beautiful green screen that hid the house from view in the summer. I cringed every time the school bus pulled up in front of our house when it was fully exposed to the street, its duct-taped windows, cracked foundation and dangerously decaying concrete steps on clear display.

With the rest of the community living in decently maintained and nicely appointed small homes — all with running water, unbroken glass in the windows and more than one bedroom — ours stood out like a sore thumb. Some kids on the bus were determined to make sure I knew it. "Oh look, we're coming up to Rosemarie's house," they'd say. "I hear they have no running water. Gross! I bet they never bathe either. There goes stinky Rosemarie into that disgusting shack. Don't touch her or you might catch something!" Such taunts were hurled at me constantly as a child, and as I grew older the bullying became even meaner and more personal.

If my father was in a bad mood, there'd be even more negative messages when I stepped through the door. He would go on the attack over minor crimes like the way I wore my hair, or even for watching a cartoon on television. "Why do you watch that garbage TV show?" he would ask. He disapproved of anything except the news or old war and history movies he liked. "Only stupid people like those shows," he'd say of the cartoons or soap operas. "You're not stupid, are you? Maybe you are, because you like watching stupid TV shows." My brother, mother and I heard these comments all the time from my father. No one stood up to him; we would all just look away as he changed the channel. Those phrases my father said to me as a child became the very same phrases that I repeated to myself in my head.

✴ CHANGING YOUR INNER VOICE

A big part of my journey toward where I am today involved dealing with all those negative words thrown at me as a child. Later on in life — and I wish it had been much earlier — I had one-on-one therapy that helped me identify that harsh inner voice and find ways to deal with it. Through that and other experiences, I have gained insights and ideas that I hope will help you deal with your own negative messages.

It can be hard to accept that we can be so harsh on ourselves. When we first become aware of this inner voice and begin to see it for what it is, the shock can sometimes trigger a whole new line of internal insults and feelings of shame. In an attempt to avoid the pain, it's understandably tempting to leave those thoughts buried in the subconscious. But clear-eyed self-awareness is a critical first step if you want to be free to move forward in your life. By really acknowledging your inner self talk and identifying the phrases that pop up again and again, you can begin to take control of the conversation.

I learned that since it's impossible to simply scrub a thought — especially a long-term habitual one — from your mind, it's imperative to deliberately replace negative phrases with positive ones. There is a saying that "what you resist persists." This means that if you are simply trying to resist a negative thought and push it away, it is quite likely to lodge itself persistently in your mind because the act of resistance is actually a form of attachment. Only by replacing that negative thought with a positive one can you alter your mindset.

You have to choose phrases that feel comfortable; lying to yourself doesn't work either. If "I did a great job" doesn't feel true, try "I did the best I could." If you're uncomfortable with phrases like "I love myself," you could say: "I am now giving myself permission to love myself and to treat myself with the respect and kindness that I deserve."

The next time you catch yourself in negative self-talk, replace those words with ones of encouragement. At first it will be difficult, like flexing a muscle you have not used for a while, but the more you do it, the easier it will become and the more comfortable you will be with accepting the new messages. After a couple of weeks of regularly using positive self-talk, there will slowly be a greater openness to even more positive and bolder affirmations. Keep going until you find you are feeling more confident and willing to take on new challenges.

Start your positive self-talk first thing in the morning, with phrases like: "Today is going to be a great day," or "I am going to do great things today," or "I feel terrific; I am going to take on today with energy and enthusiasm." You'll find yourself seeing things in a more positive light, which will affect how you react to whatever the day brings. Even the smallest adjustment in your outlook will alter the trajectory of your life.

I'm a fan of affirmations — repetitive positive statements aimed at changing your mindset for the better. But you have to be purposeful and systematic to make them work for you. One way is to write 10 different positive statements, such as "I love myself" and "This is going to be an amazing day" on small sticky notes and put them up around the house where you'll see them as you go about your daily activities. Repeat each phrase three times, as it takes repetition to alter the conversation in your mind. Your bathroom mirror is a great place to stick a loving, positive note to yourself. Imagine what a powerful boost it would be to start every day with the words, "I am a beautiful person and I deserve all the love and beauty that life has to offer."

◉ EMBRACE WHERE YOU ARE TODAY

When you're dreaming of a better life, it's easy to focus on all the things you haven't achieved yet, but it's important to remember what you have already accomplished and to appreciate your own wonderful personal qualities. Our minds are quick to add up our flaws or shortcomings, but you can train yourself to pay the same attention to your strengths.

Being proud and appreciative of your accomplishments is part of believing in yourself, and will give you more strength to deal with whatever comes your way. And being thankful for what you have will encourage more to come into your life.

Here's an exercise to help with that:

Write down what you feel are your best qualities and greatest accomplishments. Include everything you can think of. Did you finish high school, or go to college? Be proud of how much money you make each year, whatever it is. It's okay to want more, but be proud of where you are today. Did you make someone feel good today? Write it down. Break your list into three categories: everyday successes such as working out or helping your child with her homework; larger life accomplishments such as landing a job or finishing a training program; and general skills and qualities, such as being a kind person or being good at math. Be bold. There are no wrong answers, so approach this from a place of love and see what unfolds on your list. Once you have this list, keep it in your nightstand and review it each night to remind yourself of your accomplishments and strengths. If you follow the steps in this book, you will find your list will grow with strengths and skills.

One aspect of embracing ourselves and appreciating our accomplishments is being able to respond graciously to compliments. It may seem like a small thing, but it says a lot about you. For some reason, I was taught to minimize praise and respond to it self-deprecatingly. If you have been given the same programming, it's time for a change. When someone praises the job you did, say, "Thank you, that means a lot to me." When someone compliments your dress, don't invalidate it with, "This old thing? I got it at the thrift store." Instead, say, "Thank you." And you could add, "You just made my day." Or "This dress is one of my favorites."

Responding to praise with phrases like "It was nothing" or "I only got this because of luck" just hurts you because it minimizes your efforts, as well as invalidating the other person's comments.

Those of us who don't feel worthy of receiving compliments will often struggle with giving them, too. Try to find one thing about each person you meet that you appreciate, and acknowledge them for it. Any such compliments must be authentic; if they don't come from the heart, they will come across as shallow and not real. But learning how to give good, sincere compliments is valuable. When you make people feel good, they want to be around you more and are more willing to go out of their way to help you.

◉ KNOW YOURSELF

Part of believing in yourself is understanding who you really are. Many people go through life with an incomplete or inaccurate self-image. They may envision themselves as having certain traits such as a positive outlook or an outgoing personality, when the people closest to them might tell a very different story. In some cases, this disconnect can be caused by low levels of self-awareness — the person simply does not see him or herself clearly. In other cases, people may indeed be describing their true nature, but the negative conversation in their head may be bringing out very different behavior in them.

During my young adult years, when I was still struggling to figure out who I really was, many negative messages from my childhood continued to affect my self-expression. I saw myself as an outgoing and positive person, but in some situations I wasn't aware of how opinionated and emotional I could get. When someone didn't agree with what I was saying and I knew I was right, I would get excessively upset, as if I felt they were discounting me because I was not good enough. Often this would infuriate me to the point where I would push so hard in a conversation that the person would walk away. Being assertive with your opinion is a good thing, especially for women because we are so conditioned to yield to others. But being a bull in a china shop and taking no prisoners is not so great. It took me a while to realize what was prompting my behavior and to learn to pick my battles.

As I grew older I found an alternative that worked much better. As soon as I could see that the other person didn't agree with my point of view and I was not going to change his or her mind, I would say, "I see your point. Not sure I agree, but I see your point," then move on to another conversation. This allowed me to save many friendships and to be more deliberate about standing my ground more assertively when I felt something important was at stake.

It's valuable to be aware of how people react to you in different situations and how you respond to them in turn. You may or may not like what you see, but understanding how you come across is another major step in taking control and living the life that you want. Do people light up when they see you or do they shut down? When you join a conversation, does it continue on in a positive way or does it tend to turn negative? Are you treated with respect in different circles or are your opinions often dismissed?

Understanding yourself includes acknowledging your personal qualities. Some, such as whether you're an introvert or extrovert, are simply due to wiring. You can't change them, so accept and appreciate them. The same goes for your natural talents. Are you good with numbers or do you shine when it comes to communication skills? I knew early on that I had a head for numbers, and following that path led me to the success I have achieved today. Whatever your natural talent, embrace it; being inauthentic will bring only stress and anxiety.

⊛ INVEST IN YOU

One of my favorite sayings is: "Knowledge is power — the more you acquire the more powerful you become."

Believing in yourself means investing time, effort and sometimes money in learning what you need to know to achieve the life you want. It can be tempting to assume that the successful people we meet are just smarter and more capable than we are. But they began as babies, just like you and me, and acquired their knowledge and skills along the way. High-achieving people invest in themselves.

Once you have identified your strengths and interests and assessed your skills, make a commitment to invest in yourself to get moving toward your goals. For anything you want to learn, there is a teacher, whether it comes in the form of a university degree, evening courses at a community center or a more experienced coworker who can show you the ropes.

Too often when we consider investing in ourselves in this way, our negative inner voice will pipe up, "I can't afford that," "It would be a waste of money," or "I can't do that at my age." Replace those thoughts with positive affirmations like: "I am smart and I deserve to invest in myself," "With the right skills, I can be as successful as anyone else in this field," and "I deserve to be successful. All I need are the tools to get there."

We all have limited time to live our lives, and if we want to use that time well, we must equip ourselves to reach our goals, whether we're aiming to make more money or simply pursue a personal interest. One thing that has stumped me my entire life is seeing people pouring their money into new cars or TV sets, yet being very cheap about paying to acquire new skills or knowledge. Investing in yourself will pay back huge dividends in the people you meet and the knowledge and confidence you gain, while the TV and car will only depreciate in value over time.

When you increase your knowledge or learn a new skill, you're preparing yourself for the next opportunity. There is a saying that "luck comes when opportunity meets preparation," and this has been borne out many times in my own life. Those people we envy who seem really lucky are likely spending a lot of time — when no one is watching — studying, learning or honing their talent so that when an opportunity comes up they can seize it. The most gifted piano players or skilled golfers spend a significant amount of time each day practicing and training. Jennifer Lopez is not just lucky; she is talented and works incredibly hard. Countless hours of practice and planning go into every show and into each album. So apply that logic to your own life. If you want a promotion at work, think about what you need to be learning to get ready for it. Stand in the future like you already have that job. What skills should you be acquiring? Where should you be putting your extra effort? If you approach it from this perspective, you will find that when the job opening comes, you'll be the most obvious choice.

Successful people don't take shortcuts, and neither should you. If you show up halfway, others will see it in your relationships, in your work and in your children. People know a shortcut when they see it and will respond accordingly. They may not say anything in that moment, but it goes into their memory bank and the next time an opportunity comes up, you may lose out — because someone simply didn't want to take a chance on you. Ask yourself: "Am I doing the best possible job that I could be doing at this moment?" It will make a big difference in how people respond to you and what opportunities open up for you.

✹ THE PAYOFFS TO BELIEVING IN YOU

The wonderful thing about being your own believer is that you don't have to wait for someone else to give you permission. Give yourself permission to not only believe in yourself, but also to pursue your dreams.

As I've found throughout my life, taking just one step forward leads to another, and success builds on success. Each new achievement built my self-belief further until I was able to accomplish things I couldn't have dreamed of in my childhood. I started by helping Mrs. Chromiak with her vegetable stand, moved on to a waitressing job where I saved my money, and used that to leave my difficult home circumstances and step by step build a highly successful career.

Once you begin that positive, upward cycle, things will start happening differently for you too. It will show up in your personal self-talk and how you feel about yourself, resulting in a positive feedback loop that will create its own momentum. You will attract more powerful people into your life because your energy will be strong, and successful people enjoy being surrounded by like-minded individuals. Opportunities will start to crop up, and that's where the magic really starts to happen. If you follow the next six lessons in this book, you will find an abundance of opportunity will come your way, and when it does, you will be ready to embrace it.

CREATE YOUR FUTURE FROM THE FUTURE

"Nobody can go back and start a new beginning,
but anyone can start today and make a new ending."

MARIA ROBINSON

Nobody talked about college in my household when I was a young girl. In fact, nobody talked about it much in the community I grew up in either. In that working man's — and woman's — world, the ultimate dream was a union job, getting through your shifts the best you could, and looking forward to the big payoff: retiring with a pension and good benefits.

I didn't know much about college except that it was where you went to become a doctor, nurse or engineer. None of those careers appealed to me, so it didn't seem relevant.

As I grew into a teenager and the question of what I would do with the rest of my life started to loom on the horizon, my father made it clear where he'd set his sights for me: right beside my mother on the packing line of the chicken processing plant, putting cut-up chicken parts into bags. Hour after hour, day after day: raw thighs and drumsticks, breasts and wings.

He ramped up the pressure during my last year of high school. "Your aunt could help you to get a job there," he said. "Once you get the job, watch yourself for a few months and then you'll get into the union and you will be set for life."

He even wanted me to give up the restaurant job where I worked 30 to 40 hours a week throughout high school. I enjoyed that job, where I took orders, made sure customers were taken care of, took cash and even helped in the kitchen with the cooking — but I knew I didn't want to do that either for the rest of my life. Far less did I want a lifelong career of bagging up chicken parts.

The battle between me and my father over the chicken-plant job was long and intense.

"You'll end up with nothing and then what will you do?" he'd say, calling me stupid and predicting that one day, I'd see he was right. "You are going find it tough to get a job with security and benefits, and when you have nothing, don't come crawling back to me," he would say again and again. I was 16 years old and at the beginning of my senior year, and it was scary to hear these things from him.

But I knew this wasn't the right path for me.

Hints of what kind of life I did want had popped up over the years. As a child, I would accompany my parents when my father dropped my mother off for her house-cleaning job. I was struck by the size and beauty of one of the homes where she worked. It belonged to an older couple who were factory owners. They travelled to sunny places for vacations, I heard, and I admired the beautiful clothes the woman wore whenever I saw her leaving the house. This was a different world from the one I knew. I was curious and I liked the sight of it.

It would have been easy to take the path of least resistance and go to work at the chicken plant. In the eyes of my family and my community, it made perfect sense. It was secure, well-paid work, and would mean a pension when I retired. But the thought of being surrounded by chicken blood and carcass trimmings for the rest of my life filled me with revulsion and made me feel tense and nauseous.

Even worse was the idea of living a life based on "just getting through the day" instead of doing something I loved. What a waste! There's nothing wrong with serving in a restaurant or packing up chicken parts — except I knew it was wrong for me. Even at a young age, I knew instinctively how important it was that my work be harmonious with who I was.

As you work toward designing and creating a better life, it is important not to allow your past to dictate your future. View the lessons you've learned and the experiences you've had as valuable resources, but don't be bound by what has gone before. For me, it was important to acknowledge my past, then put it on the shelf, where I could access it as needed while standing in my vision for the future. When you do this, you have a clean, open slate to work with, so the possibilities are endless and exciting.

Although I was born and raised in a poor blue-collar family, that didn't mean I had to stay in that world forever. I knew my parents' lives were not what I wanted, even though I wasn't sure exactly what I did want. Because I couldn't build my future on the past, I knew I'd have to go forward and create my future from my future.

✳ BATTLING THE NAYSAYERS

Your vision for your life has to be your own. No one has the right to determine it for you. Following some-one else's ideas will lead to a big gap where fulfillment should be. You probably won't be successful either, because you'll always be battling yourself.

Some people have to battle for the right to become artists or carpenters instead of the doctors or lawyers their parents dreamed of. In my case, I had to fight to climb the socio-economic ladder. It may seem illogi-cal, but in some communities, the desire for success can be frowned upon and judged as selling out to materialism.

Whether you're being pushed up or down the socio-economic scale, it's hard to go for your dreams —

or even figure out what they might be — when you have no support from those around you. Some people simply give up when they're not in an environment that encourages and motivates them.

My decision to go against popular wisdom aroused sentiments like: "You'll never do that — you don't have any experience in that field," or "Why would you want to go there and take something like that when you can get a secure job with good pay and benefits?"

There were those who thought it wasn't quite respectable to seek wealth, and equated success with shallowness. "Money is the root of all evil," I was constantly reminded. And people said: "I would rather be poor and happy than rich and miserable." These statements made no sense to me: I knew plenty of poor people who weren't very happy.

Money may not buy you happiness but it will give you freedom, and there is nothing wrong with that, as long as it is pursued from a place of love and purpose. Success will not turn you into a shallow, selfish or unkind person, but limiting your potential in order to protect others' insecurities will make you frustrated, unhappy and maybe even bitter.

If you want to create a better life for yourself, you have to give yourself permission to acknowledge what truly gives you joy in your heart and not allow yourself to be held back by other people's limitations.

◉ ENVISIONING YOUR FUTURE

You have only one life to live, so do what you really want with it. You have the ability to create a life that gets you excited about jumping out of bed every morning; a life that makes you feel valued and worthy, that makes you feel alive and enables you to enjoy each day as if it is your last.

If you've never felt that way before, it's important to spend some time thinking about the things that inherently make you happy. Sometimes we think we know what makes us happy but when we look deep into our soul, we might find that our greatest joy comes from something else. Give yourself permission to be honest and open to your truth even if the result is not what you expected or think it should be.

Be bold with your ideas and desires, and don't allow yourself to be held back by judgmental attitudes toward your chosen path. There are many negative stereotypes for every aspect of every career, so choosing a certain job or path in life to avoid criticism is a futile waste of your time. You can't please everyone, so if you're going to be criticized for your choices, you might as well make sure they are ones you can stand by and that bring you happiness and fulfillment.

So the question becomes, "How do I know what will really give me joy and happiness?"

The good news is that no matter how confused you might feel today, the answers are all inside you, waiting to be heard. You can tap into them any time by simply becoming still and receptive and asking the right questions. But before you begin, it's important to be in a receptive frame of mind.

It is much easier to attract positive thoughts and create the energy needed to move these thoughts forward when you have a positive mindset. When you are frustrated and angry, you will only have more frustrated and angry thoughts. So begin with a clear slate, a joyful and content frame of mind, and in a peaceful, uncluttered environment.

You might want to go for a relaxing walk in the park and sit on a bench. Gaze at a peaceful water feature and allow the thoughts to freely come and go. Think about a time when you felt great joy. Was it hearing your child or spouse say, "I love you?" Was it seeing the smile on your child's face when he or she accomplished a task? Maybe you felt joy in receiving a compliment or in the look of gratitude from someone you were helping.

All along your journey to success, it will be extremely important to be able to put your mind in that state of joy. Tapping into these memories is one of the best ways to do that. It is only when you free your mind of negative energy and fill it with joy that you'll have true access to the imagination that will help you create your future.

✸ CALLING FORTH THE DREAM

Once you are in a state of relaxed joy, examine your life as it is today. Think about activities you enjoy so much that they feel effortless. What are you doing, and who are you surrounded by in those moments? What are the people around you doing? What do their faces look like? What are they wearing?

Now project yourself forward in time, and ask yourself what would get you out of bed every morning feeling alive and turned on about life. What would you be doing that would make you excited about the challenges and opportunities that lie ahead? Imagine it vividly as though it's all around you. What specifically are you doing that is bringing you joy? Are you in a certain industry, working with your hands, guiding others, or working independently on a creative project? What does your family look like? Think about every aspect of the life that you want in your ideal future. Try to envision as much detail as possible, and write it all down.

Your past can offer many clues to your ideal future. Think back to when you were a child; the things you loved to focus on and spend time doing. What did you dream about? What did you want more than anything? What made you happy?

Keep a journal and write down all the things that bring you joy and all the things that made you happy as a child. A pattern will start to emerge, giving you indications about the kind of life you need to create. It may not show you your exact career path, but it will reveal the types of environments that make you happy. From there, you can determine the kind of career that would fit into those parameters.

As a child, I drew pictures of beautiful dresses. I enjoyed watching beauty pageants and pretending to wear beautiful clothes. Even though most of my own clothes were old, stained hand-me-downs usually two sizes too big, I was allowed to play dress-up in some of my mother's clothes. She'd let me use the two dresses she wore when she first met my father, her one pair of high-heeled shoes that she never wore anymore, and a couple of sheer head scarves that served as princess veils in my fantasy world.

Playing "store" with my brother was another favorite. We'd put prices on cans of food, make pretend money from cardboard, then spend hours shopping and selling. My brother would usually be the shopper and I the cashier — a role I was able to start playing for real at Mrs. Chromiak's vegetable stand when I was seven years old. No wonder I ended up in office environments where I could not only work with numbers every day, but do it while wearing beautiful clothes!

Once you've gathered inspiration from your childhood self, look back on your various careers or jobs and think about them in a new way. Which ones gave you the most satisfaction, and what exactly was it about them that you enjoyed? Was it the people you were with, or the specific tasks you were performing? Was it because you were in a busy environment with lots of people, or were you enjoying working on your own? Some of us are wired to enjoy working in a group, while others do their best work in solitude. Neither is better than the other; the important thing is to home in on exactly which qualities and work environments make you feel good.

At first you will have to be very purposeful when trying to access this place of internal vision. Set aside time to get into a mindset free of clutter and distractions. Each time you do this exercise, write down what you envision in as much detail as possible. Keep those lists in a file or safe place and repeat this exercise daily if you can, or at least twice a week for four weeks. Over that time, the mental picture of your better life will start to become clearer.

The mere act of taking honest stock of your own preferences will help create a clear image in your mind of your ideal situation, which in turn will bring you closer to realizing it. After all, how can you choose a life path if you don't understand what you really want?

This is the time to dream big. Go outside your comfort zone. Don't let your fear of failure — or of success — get in the way. If you want to be a Grammy Award-winning songwriter, then write it down. If you want to have your own consulting business specializing in fitness, go for it! The sky is the limit, as long as you keep the focus on what makes you happy, not what looks good on paper or sounds sensible. This is the path to becoming one of those people who say, "I am so lucky because I get to do what I love every day for a living and it doesn't seem like work to me."

The next part of the exercise will help integrate your vision of your future with your overall life purpose. Like Scrooge guided by the Ghost of Christmas Yet to Come in Charles Dickens' *A Christmas Carol*, you'll be envisioning how people will remember you when you are gone from this life.

Again, close your eyes and stand in your future, but this time, think about what you'd like to leave behind in people's minds. Do you want to be remembered as a kind and generous person? As someone who changed the world? As a kind, loving grandma who enabled her family to live the lives they wanted? Or will people think of you as someone who, like Steve Jobs, made a difference in a certain industry? Project yourself far into the future and look back on what kind of life you had. What did you do for a living? Who was around you, and what are they saying about you now that you are gone?

This is an amazingly effective way to uncover your secret, subconscious yearnings, the sense of purpose that already lives inside you. You don't have to invent it; you only have to allow it to come to the surface and make itself known.

This is the point at which a lot of people lose their nerve. With a big, happy, audacious life blazing in your mind's eye, it's easy to fall back down to earth hard when you realize the size of the gap between where you want to be and where you are now. You might feel bad that it's taken so long to find your vision. You might be tempted to give yourself a hard time for not being closer to your goal. I gently urge you to give yourself a break.

Of course you have work to do, but this is not a reason to shrink your dream! You've made certain choices in the past, and you can make different ones now that you have a better idea of your goals.

Giving yourself permission to be human and flawed opens the door for learning and opportunity. If you need a certain skill, simply work toward developing it. As long as you're focused on where you want to go, anything is possible.

Well, almost anything. There are limits, but there are also imaginative alternatives. For example, I'm a female in my mid-40s, so it would be unrealistic for me to dream of becoming a player in the NHL. I could play on a women's league, though, and enjoy the experience of playing the sport I love. But if I absolutely loved NHL hockey, I could find other ways of getting into that world. I could work in a promotions department or become a sports reporter. I could go into sports medicine and work toward becoming the team physician. I could even acquire the business skills necessary to become my local team's general manager. Aim high and find a role that uses your natural skills and aptitudes in the areas you are passionate about.

If you love fashion and want to be in the fashion industry, then go for it. So what if you're not 5′10″? Maybe you'll never be a supermodel, but there are many other jobs in that world that could use your skills and might be just as rewarding. For example, how about a position as executive at a cosmetics company, an editor at a high-fashion magazine, or a clothing designer?

The voice of your heart is very different from the voice of the inner critic. While your heart whispers words of encouragement, the critic is all doom and gloom. When that inner voice says, "You can't do that," "You are not smart enough," or "You don't know anything about that," acknowledge it and say, "Thank you for sharing" followed by, "I am focusing on these goals. These are my goals and my objectives, and I know what I need to do in order to keep driving toward them."

Then return to that quiet place of love and joy, and replace the negative messages with thoughts of happiness. If it helps, add your positive affirmations. "I can do that." "I deserve to be happy." "I deserve to create a life that I love."

By diligently using this technique whenever that inner critic pops up, you will effectively cause it to disappear. If you ignore or resist it, it will persist. Negative messages lose power and dissipate when you hear them out and actively put your attention on positive ones.

Expressing the truth of who you are and what you want in life will have a beautiful side-effect: Your heart will open and more love will flow through you. You will attract more love and joy. If you want to be loved, then be lovable. Love everything around you. Give the love you wish to receive, not only to your partner and your children but also to yourself.

As you start moving toward your goal, your life will pick up momentum and take on a certain velocity. Encouraged by the "signs" you see everywhere, you will want to do it all and have it all, right now. Instead of having to work up the courage or energy to get going, you may find it's a challenge to slow down and focus on the here and now. Have patience, take it one step at a time. The journey has just begun and your destination is waiting for you.

MAP OUT YOUR PLAN

"Inch by inch, anything's a cinch"

BRIAN TRACY

Once you've decided what your future is going to look like, the next thing is to map out your plan. Any large goal can seem overwhelming at times, but if you break it down into small bite-sized pieces and focus on one step at a time, you can and will get there.

As my high school years went along, I became more and more determined to get away from that three-room shack and the ridicule and disrespect I felt because of my circumstances.

By the age of 16, I had set myself some major goals. Within 20 years, I wanted to be living in a nice house with running water. Not only would it be a nice house, it would be one of the best around. I wanted to have a job with an important role and to be well respected by my colleagues. I wanted to have enough money that I would never have to worry about paying the bills. I wanted to have nice things; I was tired of always being the one who sat by empty-handed while other kids got toys and new bikes. I had noticed the boys in the neighborhood ooh and ahh anytime a

Corvette drove by, so I promised myself that I would buy myself a Corvette by the time I was 25. As it turned out, my likes and desires changed over the years, so I never did get that Corvette. But I did buy myself a red Porsche 944 Turbo at the age of 24. It was a few years old when I got it, but it was a beautiful car, and I loved it and the success it represented.

My better life was crystal clear in my mind, but I knew it wouldn't happen on its own. To get it underway, I set out very methodically to create "My Plan."

I had already decided I wanted to move to Winnipeg, which was about 40 kilometers away. I wanted to work in a setting where people were educated, wore nice clothes and were respectful to each other. I also knew that if I wanted to get more out of my life, I'd have to figure out how to get a post-secondary education that would earn me a higher income than a worker at a chicken packing plant. All together it looked like a tall order, so to make it more manageable, I broke down every item into small individual steps.

When mapping out your plan, it helps to start with what you want to have achieved by the end of your life, then work backward to plot all the milestones along the way from there to where you are now. If you are young, those milestones will be far apart — you might count back in ten-year increments, from 80 to 70 and so on. If you're older, you can still gain value from this process by plotting your milestones in smaller periods of just a few years. The important thing is to recognize that at every stage of life, we can set goals and work systematically toward them.

By retirement age, I wanted to have owned several beautiful houses, taken many trips to wonderful destinations, had several nice cars and to have had a loving family. Working backward from there, by age 35 I wanted to have that nice house, great job and no financial worries. I knew if I was going to achieve that, then by age 25 I needed to have completed my post-secondary education. By then I would have to be living in the city where there were more of these types of jobs available. Continuing to work backward, I saw that by age 20, I would have to be working on my professional credentials, but I also knew I would need a job to support myself at the same time. I had no safety net, so failure was not an option. Going even further backward, I knew that by the age of 17, I would have to finish high school with good math and science marks in order to get into that post-secondary educational program, whatever it might be.

The details will look different for everybody, but the process is the same. Let's say, for example, that a 25-year-old grocery clerk decides she wants to be vice president of marketing in her company by the age of 50. She'll have to figure out what tools she needs in order to to start creating the life she wants. She'll probably find she'll need a college degree either in business, marketing or another relevant field. If she doesn't have money, she'll have to figure out how to support herself and pay for her education at the same time, perhaps with a student loan or a part-time job. She will also need to draw up a budget so she knows exactly what her monthly expenses will be and what monthly income she will need to cover herself.

So, working backward, in order to be the vice president of marketing by the age of 50, at 45 she would need to be a director of marketing. By 40 she would need to be in the marketing department and making significant contributions. By 30 she would need to have completed her degree and have worked on some great projects. At the age of 29 she would be in her final year of college finishing up her marketing degree. At ages 26, 27 and 28 she would be focusing on getting good grades and working part-time. And at the age of 25, where she is now, she needs to be researching colleges in her area and applying for student loans. Breaking it down this way suddenly makes what seemed like a daunting undertaking a realistic possibility.

It's important to do this working-backward exercise with every aspect of your life. As you take on each individual step along the way, you will find that long-term goal that once seemed so unreachable isn't far off after all, and before you know it, you are well on your way.

I knew that in order to create my better life I would have to save as much as I could, so while I was earning money at my high-school waitressing job, I made a conscious effort to spend it only on the things I absolutely needed. I bought all my own clothes and toiletries, but kept my wardrobe small and only spent money on what I knew I would use. The rest of my money I put into my savings account. At that time the interest rates were quite high and it was very rewarding to see my money grow each month with the 15 percent interest that it would earn.

I did everything I could to bring myself closer to my goals. I talked to my regular customers and friends about my plans. I read the want ads in the newspapers to see what types of jobs were available in Winnipeg, and I thought hard about how I was going to continue my education after high school.

Because I had already set my plan in motion, I was tuned into any information that would help move it forward. My 'eureka' moment came at my high school's career fair.

Sitting on the bleachers in the gymnasium with the 65 other twelfth graders, my attention was focused on the center floor, where one dark suit after another stepped up to present his or her profession and offer advice on how to pursue a career in their fields. First came an engineer, and then a doctor, but I wasn't interested. Next came a dark-haired man in a dark blue suit who carried himself like he was important. He said he was a certified management accountant (CMA) and was here to tell us what it was like to do his job.

My curiosity was piqued; this was an option worth considering. I was good in math and got high marks in high school accounting so I knew numbers were my forte. When he told us it was possible to earn an accounting designation at night school, I knew at that point that was the path I was going to take. I would work during the day and study at night. Every business needed an accountant, which meant there would be a certain level of security in that profession. My decision was made. As soon as the speakers had finished their presentations, I hurried down the steps of the bleachers to speak with this important-looking man and get every bit of information I could about becoming a CMA, a designation that has recently been changed to chartered professional accountant, or CPA.

The next step was to find a post-high school job. I knew from researching the accounting program that I needed practical experience in order to get my designation, so I focused on accounting-related jobs, asking everyone I knew for advice or referrals. I'd often discussed my career goals and aspirations with Bill Auger, a regular customer at the greasy spoon, who surprised me one day by offering me a job at a farm-parts place in Winnipeg, where he worked. "I need an inventory clerk and could use a hard worker who is good with numbers," he said. I could hardly believe it; I now had a job to go to after I finished high school. My plan was starting to line up. It almost seemed too good to be true. It was my first solid evidence that when you commit yourself to a goal, the world around you will shift in the slightest of ways to help you achieve it.

Even though things seemed to be falling into place beautifully, I sometimes had to fight my inner voice telling me that I couldn't do it, that I wasn't smart enough or that I was never going to pull it off. Sometimes I wondered if I should bow to my father's wishes after all and just go to work at the chicken packing plant.

I had no one to help me through these moments so when the inner doubt was particularly strong, sometimes I would go for a walk or find a peaceful place to sit where I could clear my head and create a more positive internal conversation. I knew that unless I made a change, I would end up just like my parents, and that thought was intolerable. So I would sit quietly, focus on my end goal and think about what my life would be like once I got there. Some might call it daydreaming, but I knew it was important. I had to be brave and bold if I wanted to be successful, so I would tell myself, "I am smart and I deserve to live a life that I love just as much as anyone else does," that "it won't be that hard" and that "I deserve to be happy just like the other people I have seen in my life." If they could do it, then so could I. I used many of the same affirmations that I shared with you in chapter one, and they helped reinforce my positive thinking and belief in myself. I couldn't always keep the inner critic silent, but I wasn't about to let it take charge of my life or stop me in my tracks.

My next task was to find a place to live in Winnipeg. After asking around, I found that one of my girlfriends also wanted to move to Winnipeg, so we decided to be roommates. On the weekends we would take my yellow Comet into the city and go apartment hunting. We started by looking at very cheap run-down apartments in bad neighborhoods. I was okay with them because almost anything was a step up from where I lived — all the apartments had running water and electric heat. But my girlfriend had different ideas. Her family home was modest, but she still had her own room and the small privileges that most young girls enjoy. She couldn't bring herself to live in one of those old run-down apartments. So we started looking at nicer two-bedroom apartments in high rises. We found one we both loved that was near a bus route we both would need for work and decided to take it. It was in a newer building and had two bedrooms, one bathroom and a decent kitchen, dining and living room area. We signed a lease, and in August of 1984 we moved in. Luckily for me, my girlfriend's parents gave her their used furniture. It wasn't fancy but it was in decent shape and meant we had nearly everything we needed.

I was nervous but excited about this new life. I spent the summer working as an inventory clerk at the farm parts store and reviewing the assigned reading in preparation for my accounting courses that would start in September. Because it was night school, I would only be doing one class at a time. My first class was basic accounting, which I had already taken in high school, earning 97 percent in the final exam. However, there was a lot of new information that I knew would take some effort to learn. By the time September rolled around, I was excited but intimidated about the beginning of classes.

Walking into the classroom on that first night, I was convinced that every one of those strangers in the room was smarter than me. I sat at the back of the classroom for the first few classes and slouched in my chair feeling very inadequate and apprehensive. I wanted to be invisible because I thought if anyone saw me, they would tell me I didn't deserve to be there. But my desire to change my life was even stronger than my nerves, so I knew I had to persevere. As I worked my way through the course, I found that in fact I was good at the work, it didn't take much for me to earn good grades, and the other students were quite nice. Eventually, my confidence grew, and I settled into a sense of belonging.

With that, I had completed the first major items in my plan. I had left Garson, found a job that was relevant to my goals, moved into an apartment in Winnipeg, and started my post-secondary education. I had already altered the trajectory of my life, although at the time I couldn't appreciate just how significantly. It's like moving the needle of a compass just one degree; the shift seems small but will eventually lead to a very different destination. I was officially on the road to my better life.

◉ GET TIME ON YOUR SIDE

We all tend to take our time for granted and think that we have an infinite supply of it. Well, we don't. If you're not careful, you can spend as much time chasing the little fish as the big fish, so make sure your priorities focus on chasing those big fish — doing things that will bring you closer to your larger goals. If you don't deliberately make time for the things that are the most important to you, it is all too easy to get caught up in day-to-day tasks. Before you know it, months have gone by and you still haven't moved any closer to your goal.

A big part of effective time management is prioritizing your tasks and managing your to-do list. Every morning, systematically write your to-do list for the day, breaking each activity down into very specific steps. I have used this technique my entire adult life.

Not only does it keep me focused on the task at hand, it also helps me to prioritize which items are most important. By writing the tasks on paper and numbering them, you are clearing your mind so you can focus on completing these tasks instead of mentally juggling all the things you need to get done. Even if your list is 30 or 40 items long, putting them down on paper means you can place them in order of priority and focus on getting them done. Always ask yourself: "Is this important and is it moving me forward to my end goal?" Give top priority to what will move you toward the life you want.

As you review the items on your to-do list, notice whether you could delegate any to others in order to free up some of your time. Ask yourself if each one is really important; you may find you can cut some off the list. Each time you complete a task, check it off. Take a few moments to enjoy the feeling of satisfaction and accomplishment each checkmark brings, and use it to help keep you motivated. It's not always easy to be so disciplined, but practicing skills like this will keep you moving forward.

Have you ever known people who are always busy but don't seem to get much done? Many times that is because they are not focusing on completion. If you want to keep up your forward momentum, you have to finish what you start. Mike Ellis, a very smart friend of mine who is president of a large us corporation, once told me that when his employees complain of being too busy, he often tells them: "Don't confuse activity with results!" Getting the job done and crossed off your list means you can give 100 percent to the next task. If you only get things half done before moving on to another task, nothing gets completed and you will go into a stall even though you are really busy.

Take on the most challenging tasks first thing in the morning when you are fresh and have the most energy. By the end of the day, these things may seem too daunting, and they will continue to be put off. Every day, try to do the top three things on your list. On days when you are very tired or distracted, at least try to do the one most important thing on your list, but it's always best to do the top three if you can. This focus will raise your confidence and keep you moving closer to your end goal.

Some days you'll just feel overwhelmed by the tasks at hand. When that happens to me, I try to get a change of scenery, maybe even take a brisk walk to clear my head. If that's not an option, I simply close my eyes at my desk, breathe deeply and visualize something that makes me feel calm. For me, it is sitting on a grass bank in the woods near a babbling brook where I can hear the water flowing and feel the warmth from the sun on my body and a light comfortable breeze blowing on my face. Once you've calmed and re-energized yourself, take another look at your list and focus on one task at a time. Trust yourself. When you have what seems to be an insurmountable mountain of things to do, break them down into bite-size pieces and you will accomplish so much more.

This technique also applies to breaking down the hours in your week so you can focus on larger goals. Say for example I need to get a college degree. What does that mean in practical terms? It means I'm going to start my course on a certain day, and I'm going to study five times a week for a total of 20 hours a week. That means I'm going to be busy studying every Sunday, Monday, Wednesday, Friday and Saturday from 4 pm to 8 pm. Looking at it this way breaks all that studying into bite-size pieces I can handle. It is important to always schedule time for these activities and make them a priority. Once your scheduled time for a task is over, move on to the next task.

When things don't go exactly according to plan, it can be difficult to know when you should rearrange your schedule to take more time for the task, and when it's better to drop it and move on with your original plan. Every situation is different. If you are very close to completing something when your scheduled time is up, you might want to keep going in order to get it done. But if the task will require more time and effort than you had expected, it's often better to stick to your schedule and move on to your next activity once your allotted time has passed, rescheduling completion of the unfinished task for another day.

You'll be more efficient and get better results if you train yourself to be completely present in whatever you're taking on. Being present means being completely aware and focused on what you are doing at any given moment. This is just as important in personal relationships with family and friends as it is with work and professional activities. When you are completely present, your relationships will be deeper and you'll be better able to accomplish tasks.

Even with the most rigorous schedule-keeping, there will be times when you aren't able to do exactly what you'd planned. Give yourself permission to not be perfect. The key is to get back to where you were before things went off-course, a place where you are calm and can take anything on. If you miss a deadline or scheduled study time, that inner voice in your head can take over and derail you from continuing on toward your goal. Don't beat yourself up; just pick yourself up, take a deep breath and keep going, perhaps visualizing your calm place if it helps eliminate the negative thoughts and replace them with positive ones.

If you tend to get bogged down often, take a look at your home and work space — it may be that you need to put your environment in order. Too much clutter around you is like clutter in your brain — it creates a kind of mental background noise that can be very distracting. It is important to get rid of the clutter to clear your head, so schedule some time to clean up. When you receive a piece of mail, read it, deal with it and then file it or throw it away. Do not leave it sitting there or promise to "get back to it later." Every time you touch that paper, you use up some of your time. If your workspace is full of paper, clear it by focusing on one piece at a time and work through the pile in front of you. Clearing your environment will make you a better time manager and improve your confidence and sense of effectiveness.

It's important to keep projecting yourself into the future and anticipating what you'll need in the time to come. Try to stay ahead of potential problems as well as sweeping up behind them. Carefully and methodically laying out your plans in advance will expose the gaps, giving you a chance to find solutions ahead of time rather than being blindsided by problems. When challenges do arise (which they will), you will be prepared to deal with them.

Any action is better than no action at all. When your body and mind are engaged and working toward your goal, you will feel energized and uplifted. It is when you do nothing that you feel weak and helpless. Our bodies and our minds are not meant to sit around and do nothing. There may be times when you're not sure if the action you are taking is the right one, but it doesn't matter. The mere act of doing something will alter your trajectory and create possibilities and move you closer to your end goal.

BUILD A NETWORK OF SUPPORTERS

"Each day when I awake I know I have one more day to make a difference in someone's life."

JAMES MANN

Now that you have a plan in place to create your better life, the most important thing to remember is that you are not alone. You may not even know it yet, but there is a whole network of people out there who will be willing to guide and support you. You may feel like you are supposed to know everything before you begin and at times you may even feel overwhelmed. But you don't have to know everything in advance. A lot of learning will come from just putting yourself out there and starting the process. As long as you open your mind to new possibilities, you will attract the knowledge and experience that you need to move forward.

Mentors, sponsors and inspirational figures are all important in your life and each will play a different role. A *mentor* is someone who will give you guidance, encouragement and practical support; someone who can help you learn the ropes in any given situation. Mrs. Chromiak was an important early mentor in my life, although I didn't know it at the time. When she showed me how to handle cash transactions, she was teaching me valuable skills that would help me in my career. And when she trusted seven-year-old me to serve her customers, she helped instill a solid foundation of confidence essential to pursuing my dreams. Her belief in me literally changed my life.

A *sponsor* is someone who advocates for you; someone who promotes you or helps you with introductions or opportunities. Sponsors will recommend you in certain situations or may create opportunities for you. Bill, my customer from the greasy spoon who got me hired at the company where he worked, is an example of a great sponsor in my life.

An *inspirational figure* is someone who makes you want to do more and do better. Such people motivate you and get you excited about your journey. They may be people you know in real life, but could just as well be celebrities or historic figures whose life stories inspire you. One of my favorite inspirational figures is Abraham Lincoln. Here's a brief timeline of the events in his life:

1809: Born
1816: Family forced out of their home; seven-year-old Lincoln had to work to help support the family
1818: Mother died
1832: Ran for state legislature and lost
1833: Store failed, leaving him debt-ridden

1834: Ran for state legislature and won

1835: Sweetheart died

1836: Suffered a nervous breakdown

1836: Re-elected to state legislature and received license to practice law

1838: Defeated for House Speaker

1840: Re-elected to Illinois state legislature

1841: Established new law practice

1843: Failed to receive nomination for us Congress

1846: Elected to Congress

1855: Failed in quest to become us Senator

1856: Defeated for nomination for vice president

1860: Elected president, eventually becoming one of the most respected presidents of the United States

The tenacity, strength and vision it must have taken for Lincoln to achieve his life goals despite his repeated failures is remarkable to me. When I was first introduced to this story I copied it out on a piece of paper and hung it up in a place where I could read it every day. Whenever I was feeling challenged by life, I would look at everything this man went through and marvel that despite all those setbacks, he went on to become one of the greatest presidents who ever lived. This story guided me through several critical points when I needed to make big decisions, and gave me courage when I struggled with my personal confidence. Even now, when I feel self-doubt creep in, I look back at Lincoln's personal history. It helps me to remember that even some of the greatest people have had to pick themselves and keep going.

Oprah Winfrey is another major inspirational figure. She faced many harsh challenges as a child, but worked her way up from news reporter to become one of the highest paid and most influential celebrities of our time. When you face a challenging situation you can always ask yourself, "What would Oprah do?" By putting your focus on her and taking it off yourself, you get a clearer picture of the situation and remove your own self-limiting beliefs and fearful emotions from the equation.

Reading biographies of the people you want to emulate can help you understand how they did what they did and start shaping your life in that direction. It can be incredibly motivating to discover they're just people like you and me, and that their achievements came from hard work and perseverance.

I have many inspirational people in my life, including Peter Thomas, a very successful businessman in Vancouver who has always lived life to the fullest. An author and motivational speaker, he has been incredibly generous with his time and spirit. Sometimes when I am facing difficult decisions, I ask myself, "What would Peter do?" and that often helps me make good decisions.

See if you can identify one or two people in your circle who are living the kind of life you want. They may not have everything exactly the way you'd like, but their example can serve as a template for you. If you want to be a successful real estate investor, look for people who are achieving that. How did they get started? What were their first projects? Study what they are doing and start emulating them. Learn how they do what they do and use that information to put your personal plan together.

☀ WELCOME YOUR HELPERS

Your mentors, sponsors and inspirational figures can help you to gather the skills, tools and resources you need to create your better life.

By the time I was 18, I had already taken numerous steps away from the life I did not want and toward the one I did. I had left the dilapidated shack and the community where I felt disrespected and had started working toward a career that could bring me the success and respect I sought.

At that point, I had been in my first apartment for a year with my girlfriend. I had changed jobs and was now working as an accounting clerk in an insurance company while taking my CMA courses at night. By taking the CMA program I was already starting to add to the skills in my tool kit. As an accountant I knew I would be respected and this would open up options for my career. I had researched the average income for accountants, and knew that if I stayed the course, one day I'd have a decent income and a nice house.

But at 18, my income was still very low. When my roommate broke the news that she wanted to move out, I wasn't sure if I wanted to keep the apartment or look for other options. My negative self-talk started to chime in and I was afraid that I wouldn't be able to find a place to live. Maybe my father had been right after all.

It was at this point that my next mentor came along, in the form of my boyfriend's mother, Olga.

She was a real estate agent and I had talked with her several times about the housing market. She always said to me, "You're better off to pay for a mortgage than to pay rent." This really got me thinking. I was paying rent every month and I knew it was money I would never get back. I had heard older married people at work talk about buying their homes and the process of buying real estate. I knew all of the houses out there had to be owned by someone, and I figured I might as well be one of those people.

I wondered what it would take for me to be able to own a house. Given that I was making about $850 a month before taxes, I asked Olga how much of a house I could afford if I brought in a roommate to pay $250 per month rent. She ran some numbers and said I could probably look at a house in the $25,000 to

$30,000 range. Intrigued, I asked if there was anything on the market like that. To my surprise, she said there was, and offered to pull some listings for me.

The next day we sat at the kitchen table as she showed me the printouts on properties in my price range. They were all small, modest houses. Some looked old and run down, but others were charming. That weekend we looked at several houses, and I found one I thought would work. It was small — about 600 square feet. It had two small bedrooms, a small kitchen, a small dining and living area, one bathroom with an original claw-foot tub, a back porch and small partial basement with an exposed dirt floor and hookups for a washer and dryer. It wasn't the nicest house on the block but it was something I could see myself owning. And it was certainly a lot nicer than the house I grew up in.

I put in an offer. It was listed for $29,000 and we offered $26,000 with several "subject to" clauses, all of which Olga explained to me in detail. I was definitely outside my comfort zone but she assured me I could back out at any time if I felt I had to.

That house purchase, and Olga's help in making it, is an example of how role models and opportunities show up in your life when you're clear on your goals. I wasn't shy about my desire to be successful and build my personal net worth. I asked questions, I was curious, and people around me noticed and offered to help. Had I been negative and closed off, or unsure of what I wanted, none of this would have happened.

Your role models and mentors will not always look like what you expect, but when you are open to possibilities, they will appear. In this case, it just so happened that my boyfriend's mother was very knowledgeable about real estate and willing to take the time to educate me on the market and how to go about buying a house. Because we had a personal relationship, I trusted her and knew she had my best interests at heart.

When opportunities like this show up, be ready to do the work necessary to decide if you should take them on. The more research you do, the more confident you'll be about making decisions. Remember, there are no shortcuts. Make a "to-do" list when researching an opportunity and dig hard into the details. It is in the details that money is made or lost. But if your research shows you should go ahead, then don't be afraid to step through the door.

I was very anxious throughout the process of buying that first house, as I had never done anything like this on my own. I spent several nights laying out a budget and making sure I had everything in order. I had $2,000 saved up, which was enough for my down payment and closing costs. I had applied for financing through the insurance company I worked for, which gave a ¾ percent discount on mortgages for employees.

After checking and double-checking to make sure I hadn't overlooked anything, I saw the numbers added up, so I went ahead and closed on the house. And just like that, my life trajectory was altered yet again.

By purchasing my first house, I had added new skills to my tool kit. At 18, I became the resident expert in real estate at my office. Within the year, the markets went up and my purchase inspired several coworkers to buy their own homes. Not only were these older colleagues following my example, they were also seeking my advice on their purchases. After a lifetime of having my opinions discounted and invalidated, it was mind-blowing to have people valuing what I had to say. And now it was my turn to mentor someone else.

Guidance and mentorship doesn't always come directly from individuals — it can also come from books and courses. By reading this book, you are exposing yourself to coaching that can help you create a better life. There are many self-help books and courses out there, and it's important to find the ones that work for you. Once you have opened your mind to new possibilities, you will be drawn to the people and the information you need most. I took several professional development courses created by the likes of Brian Tracy, Zig Ziglar and Dale Carnegie, author of *How to Win Friends and Influence People*. Each of these courses gave me new skills and insights to add to my tool kit.

In the early years of my career, I was very aware of my weak social skills in professional settings. I had never been taught appropriate behavior and correct protocol when meeting people in a professional environment. I didn't even know proper table manners. To compensate for this, I watched successful people interact and paid close attention to their mannerisms, how they spoke to each other and handled themselves in various situations in order to learn from them and emulate them. But I still lacked confidence because none of this was natural for me.

When I first moved to Winnipeg, I had seen an ad for a modeling course at John Casablancas Institute in the newspaper. I was interested in modeling, so I signed up. Walking on a ramp in front of complete strangers at the age of 17 was absolutely terrifying for me, but I now see it as one of the best things I did for myself; an important step toward building my confidence and learning how to carry myself in public.

By the age of 19, I was doing a bit of professional modeling on the side, as well as working at the insurance company, where I was then in the real estate accounting department. Although modeling had boosted my confidence in front of people, I was still terrified to speak in front of a group. I knew I was going to have to conquer this fear if I wanted to be successful in my career, so I decided to address it head on.

Toastmasters is an international organization that helps people master the art of public speaking. Members get an opportunity to practice speaking skills in a safe and constructive environment at regular meetings. I was fortunate that the company I worked for had an internal Toastmasters group that met over the lunch hour once a week. Admission to the group was by invitation only, so in order to join it, I needed a sponsor. I asked my boss's boss if he would sponsor me to join the group. I had always been so intimidated by people with authority, so when I approached him I was incredibly nervous. My hands got clammy and I started to sweat as the tension mounted in my body. The little voice inside my head taunted me: What did I think I was doing, asking someone who was so much more important than me for a favor? But I did it anyway, and to my great surprise he smiled and said, "Absolutely." I was shocked by how easy it was, and very surprised that someone would actually agree to do something to help me.

For the first couple of meetings I just watched the others, and then it was my turn to give my first speech — a talk about myself. There was a specific format and set of guidelines to follow. I had to talk about my upbringing, my background and explain some of my personal beliefs. I was so embarrassed about the environment I'd grown up in that I decided to avoid any direct reference to my house or my family, and instead talk more about the town I'd lived in and the schools I attended. I would talk about my goals of becoming a CMA and getting into management one day. I would also speak about my house purchase, and about self-limiting beliefs and how they could thwart people in realizing their goals and dreams.

I was terrified, but up to the stand I went. As I began, my hands shook so badly I could hardly read my notes. I forgot most of the speech and ended up trying to read it from the shaking papers. Beads of sweat formed on my forehead; all I wanted was to walk away from the podium and just have it be over. With each word, I got more and more caught up in my head, until my thoughts about how badly I was doing almost paralyzed me. I had to push on to just get through the speech that I already knew was a disaster. I was certain that when I finished, I would be torn apart by the others. Part of me expected them to ask me to leave the group because my speech was so bad. I was demoralized and terrified.

As with every other speech I had watched being delivered at Toastmasters, the group followed a formal format in giving feedback. One person would facilitate the conversation while others gave their feedback one at a time. As I sat there almost ready to break into tears, it took everything I had to hold it all in and act professionally. To my great surprise and relief, the feedback was very constructive and shared in a supportive way. There were comments like, "Initially when you got up you had a very nice presence, but I noticed your hands shaking. Try to take deep breaths and maybe try to memorize the material next time so you won't need to rely on your notes." Another person said he remembered his first speech and how difficult it was, and congratulated me on having the courage to do it. I was so used to being ridiculed when I did something wrong that it was foreign to me to receive constructive criticism. Although I was emotionally exhausted from the experience, I knew my life would be changed forever as a result of taking part in this group. Part of me still wanted to quit and not deal with it again but the bigger part knew I couldn't. I had started something I knew I had to continue no matter how uncomfortable it was.

As time went on, I put in a lot of effort to do the work required for the speeches. Each time I got up in front of the group it got easier, until I reached the point where suddenly I realized I quite enjoyed public speaking. I continued on with that Toastmasters group for the next year, and it was one of the best things I did at that company. Not only did my public speaking skills improve immensely, I also built solid relationships with some very senior people in the company. Plus, the experience gave me significant insights into battling my negative self-talk and the value of mentors.

This was my first experience of networking with influential people. Because we were in a mutually supportive group, our connections were genuine and natural, and I particularly looked up to one very successful and beautiful older woman named Nancy. Over time, as I got to know the people in the group, I was able to ask advice on career decisions. I felt very supported, even though I was by far the most junior person there. Developing relationships with these people was important to building my own confidence and realizing that if they could be successful, then so could I. Not only did I see the benefit of creating a great support network with this group, I also saw it as a wonderful opportunity to grow mentally and emotionally.

If you want to surround yourself with successful people and build relationships in the right circles, you must start putting yourself in the places that you would find these people. For example, if you are interested in business, you could join the Chamber of Commerce or other industry-specific networking groups. If you want to learn about private equity and funding, look for local angel investing groups (these are groups of individuals who put money into start-up companies) and find out if you can intern with them. If you want to meet and get to know successful people, start attending galas and fundraisers. If you can't afford to pay to attend these events, offer your support as a volunteer. If you want to get into the fashion industry, look for industry conferences and fashion shows, and find a way to attend, if not as a guest then as an intern or volunteer. Go to all of the networking events you can — really put yourself out there. When you attend these events, don't be afraid to share your dreams and goals because there may be someone there who is inspired by you and will offer you help along the way.

Also, don't be afraid to accept the kindness of strangers. When someone offers to make an introduction, say "yes, and thank you" and, more importantly, follow up. There will be times you follow up and get no response, but there will also be times that the offer is genuine and the person comes through. Those few occasions can open opportunities for you that you never dreamed of.

One of my biggest regrets in life came when I was about 20 years old. By then I had moved up in the insurance company to the internal audit department. I was on my first business trip, to do an audit at the company's office in Montreal. It was my first time flying in an airplane, and I was elated about the trip. I was out for dinner with my boss on the first night when a man approached us, walking over from a table of about ten very businesslike diners. He slid his card across the table toward me, looked at me and said, "Mademoiselle, you are very beautiful. I work for L'Oreal cosmetics and I would like you to come in and do a test shoot to model for us."

I had always dreamed of being a cosmetics model. I would look at those beautiful women in glossy magazines and wish I could be one of them. But when the opportunity arose, my own insecurities and negative self-talk took over.

There I was, sitting across the table from my boss, who was not a very nurturing person and seemed annoyed by the whole thing. In that moment, I was terrified about losing my job. I feared I could get fired if she thought I was interested in doing something else. It was my own insecurities and negative self-talk that made me determined not to show any interest in the man's offer. Sadly I left his business card on the table when we left the restaurant, just to demonstrate to my boss that I was focused on my job and not looking elsewhere.

I regret it to this day. It may not have amounted to anything, but then again it might have. Here was a perfect stranger offering me the possibility of what would have been my ultimate dream job and I turned it down. Years later, I reflected on that moment and decided I would never again pass up an opportunity I really wanted, no matter how awkward or uncomfortable the circumstances around it might be. That decision has enabled me to take advantage of opportunities when they arise; in fact, it's one of the reasons I am writing this book.

◉ APPRECIATE YOUR MENTORS

When you are open and receptive to help, your mentors, sponsors and guides will always show up. Come to expect them and you will never be disappointed. When they appear, it is important to treat these relationships as precious and be grateful for them. Always be respectful of your mentor's time. If you are supposed to meet at one o'clock, make sure you are there on time. In fact, it's a good idea to plan to be 20 minutes early. When people show up late to meetings, the message I get is that they do not respect my time, ergo they do not respect me. Follow through on your mentors' advice, and update them on the results. If they've made an introduction or set up a meeting for you, let them know how it went. When people put themselves out for you and you do not follow through, you're telling them their help is unappreciated, so they are unlikely to extend themselves again. Acknowledge them and thank them for helping you because chances are they have a busy life and could be spending their time doing other things.

Accepting support is easier when you understand where it's coming from. Many people who have achieved a level of success really do want to help other people become successful too. They like passing along their knowledge and wisdom and may find it especially exciting if they happen to see themselves in you. Chances are that they too received support when they were starting out and now want to give back, which we talk more about in lesson seven.

So be open to possibility and enjoy these very special relationships that benefit both sides. We all need a little help along the way, and when you accept that support graciously and gratefully, you are taking another step toward creating your better life.

SET YOURSELF UP FOR SUCCESS

"There is no passion to be found in playing small — in settling for a life that is less than the one you are capable of living."

NELSON MANDELA

No matter how great your plan or awesome your potential new future, it will be hard to achieve without a supportive environment. Many other things in your life will try to pull you in different directions and it's easy to be distracted and lose sight of your dreams. Putting a support structure in place for your mental, emotional, and physical well-being is essential if you're going to keep moving forward on your journey.

In the previous chapter, we saw how important it is to find and surround yourself with mentors, sponsors and inspirational figures, but it doesn't stop there. You need to be surrounded in all aspects of your life by people who support and believe in you. Nowhere is this more important than in close personal relationships.

We would like to believe that our family and friends have our very best interests at heart. After all, these are the people who love us, who know us best, and have walked through life with us. These people are our "tribe." They are a part of our identity, as we are part of theirs. Naturally we all want success for each other, right? A win for one is a win for all.

If you are lucky enough to have truly supportive loved ones who can dream and grow along with you, you are blessed with a great gift. Unfortunately, most of us have some people in our inner circle who take a less positive approach.

There are bound to be those in your life who do not share your dream. Your family and friends have always known you to be a certain way, and maybe they liked things the way they were. When you take on new challenges and follow new dreams, you may suddenly seem different, and they might be quite uncomfortable with the changes. Through misplaced protectiveness or even jealousy, they may try to rein you in.

My father was a case in point. He was critical of my efforts to get away from home and obsessed with his idea that I should work at the chicken processing plant where I could make nine dollars an hour, join the union and get benefits.

All through my senior year in high school, my father lectured me about it, insisting I was making a huge mistake. When I told him I wanted to do my accounting courses, at first he said that was a mistake too. Later, when he could see how determined I was, he came around to suggesting that I work at the chicken plant while taking my CMA courses. I explained that in order to earn my accreditation, I had to be working in accounting, not at a factory, but this was so outside of his frame of reference, he just couldn't envision such a life.

While my father's efforts could be seen as an attempt to help and protect me, I believe there was a darker side to it. I think his insecurity about his own limited education and lack of accomplishment made him feel personally insulted by my ambition. He took my rejection of the chicken plant as a rejection of him. He interpreted my choices as disrespectful, and sometimes, in the period before I left home, this would make him so angry that he would work himself into a frenzy and lash out at me verbally and physically.

I was changing and my father was losing control. He wasn't able to see the future I wanted to create for myself; he was so stuck in his own self-limiting beliefs and insecurities that he just couldn't see past them. The only way he felt he could regain his say over me was through attacks and strong-arm tactics.

His constant browbeating did get me down. It made me question myself, and wonder whether I was making the right decision. If I had been a little less determined by nature, or if I had not been so single-mindedly focused on my goals, my life could easily have worked out very much for the worse.

The day I left home in my yellow Comet, my father and I had a big fight. He told me to not come crawling back to him when I lost my job. He even accused me of taking money from him. I was very upset and shaken by the exchange and did not talk to my father for a year afterwards.

My relationship with my mother was equally toxic but in a different way. She never understood the work I did, and with her limited intellectual capacity, it was hard to talk about anything significant going on in the world. When we talked by phone after I left home, our conversations were nothing more than her using me as a negative dumping ground. She gossiped about the neighbors, talked about who was sick and dying, and complained about my father and her home life. I would usually answer the phone in a positive mood, but by the time I hung up I'd be frustrated and tense, like someone had sucked the life out of me. I began dreading the calls because they felt like a barrage of negativity. Finally, I asked my mother if we could please just talk about something positive. At this, she became very quiet and had almost nothing to say. She had spent her whole life focusing on the negative, and no one ever challenged her on it. Positivity was a muscle she had never used before, and she was not ready or able to learn how.

My mother was an early lesson about negative people, who can show up anywhere, including in friendships and working relationships. There will always be people who view others as just ears to dump problems into. They'll be in much better spirits at the end of such encounters — while their unfortunate listeners will have any positive energy sucked right out of them. Avoid these relationships because they will only bring you down and drain your energy. And make sure you're not one of those doing the dumping. When negative thoughts enter my mind, I simply say to myself, "This is not a thought I want in my head. I am going to replace you with another thought."

As my dealings with my parents showed, some familial relationships are unhealthy, even toxic.

People like me, who want to do things our families can't understand, get messages like: "Why would you waste your time with that?" "Why do you have to go to that networking thing? There is nothing for you there — everything you need is right here," or even, "Are you just going there to use people?"

If you feel attacked or undermined in your family, it's important to know you do not have to accept criticisms or browbeating. You can choose where and with whom you spend your time. Some family members may be unhealthy people with hurtful intentions. Others may be acting out of insecurity or low self-esteem. Either way, it is okay to minimize your exposure to them. It isn't easy when they come from the heart of your family, but it's essential, especially while your confidence is fragile. If you don't limit your contact, these relationships will zap your energy and kill your desire to improve your future.

For this reason, I chose to limit my interactions with my family for quite a long time. It wasn't until I started to achieve my own success that I was able to reach out and try to build a relationship on a new foundation. It was hard to reopen myself to them at first, but I found it helpful to simply acknowledge them for who they were. I reminded myself that my father was insecure and scared, and that my mother had limited capacity and didn't know any better. By this point, I could be more tolerant of their behavior and felt less susceptible to being dragged down by it.

Examine all the relationships in your life — with friends, colleagues, family members, lovers or partners — and ask yourself how they make you feel. If you find any one of these relationships is not making you feel worthy, loved and fulfilled, ask yourself why you are still in it.

Sometimes a little communication can make a big difference. If your spouse regularly makes statements that make you feel bad about yourself or limited in your potential, tell him or her how that makes you feel. If you don't get anywhere with that, seek professional support from someone who can help guide the conversation. Making big shifts in your personal relationships is never easy, but it is important to try. This is not something that one person can turn around on his or her own — both people in the relationship have to be willing to change. Knowing you have done your best and given your partner the opportunity to grow with you can make it easier to see when it might be time to move on and look for a more supportive relationship.

Never settle for relationships that make you feel like you are number two, and be prepared to walk away from those that do. Do not allow yourself to be treated as an afterthought; not only your present sense of well-being but your entire future depends upon it.

All too often, women become emotionally invested in romantic relationships far sooner than men. If you are one of those women who becomes emotionally invested as soon as you are intimate with a man, consider waiting until you have gone out for a few months and have had a conversation about being exclusive before you get intimate. In my opinion, if you are looking for a committed relationship it's smart to hold off on the sex and wait until you have established a strong enough bond and friendship that he will want to be exclusive with you. If he is not willing to give you that, then move on. Don't get caught up in the talk that there are no good men available. I think the opposite is true: there are a lot of great guys out there, and you deserve one who is able and willing to give you what you need.

Be positive and focus on your plan and you will be amazed by who shows up for you. As you raise the quality of your life you will naturally attract a higher caliber of partner. In the meantime, take it slow while you are dating. Be patient with these relationships; they will form over time, and if the other person wants to see you again he or she will certainly call or text. If you do not hear from him or her, move on. There is nothing more damaging to your self-esteem than trying to connect with someone romantically, but getting nothing back or short messages that make excuses. When you hold yourself in high regard, that message is transmitted to others. It is also important to hold onto your own interests and passions, the things you're proud of and love to talk about, whether it's children, work, art or sports.

When you change, your life will change too. Positive people love being surrounded by other positive people. People who are creating success are more open and have a more positive perspective. As you become more positive and successful yourself, you'll attract more and more of these people into your life.

◉ RELY ON YOURSELF

People who say, "I'm going to win the lottery," or "I'm going to find a husband to take care of me," are making a big mistake. In both cases, they're giving away their power to chance.

As far as husbands go, let me tell you something about high-quality men: They don't want a woman who is not going to carry her own weight. Some may prefer their wife to stay home and take care of the family once children arrive, but they want to know their wives are going to contribute to the relationship one way or another. If you are looking for a good-looking millionaire mate, then you had better be prepared to be an equal match.

And do not think that having your boyfriend's baby is a good way to keep him. By inviting an "accidental" pregnancy, you are only setting yourself up for a life of hard work and sacrifice. Children are beautiful gifts, and even better when you have a plan in place to provide for and take care of them. If the father of an unplanned child chooses to be involved, you are fortunate, but if he chooses not to, you have put yourself in a situation where you are responsible for another life and all the added stresses that come with that. Plan your future — don't just let it happen in an uncontrolled way.

If you do find yourself on your own with children, it's even more important that you find a way to increase your value in the workforce by adding to your skill set. This will enable you to earn more money and provide a better life for yourself and your children.

◉ UNDERSTAND YOUR EMOTIONS

We are all emotional beings. Emotions bring us our greatest joys and our deepest sorrows, but it is easy to let them run away on us, sometimes without any basis in fact. It's helpful to know how to deal with this common pitfall in human interactions if you want to gain control of your life and retain your power.

The key is to determine the facts before allowing yourself to get emotional about something. Here's an example: Imagine that a young man asks a girl out to a picnic. He is imagining sun, romance, a blanket on the grass, and getting to know this beautiful girl. She is thinking of ants, cold wet ground and shivering, so she says "no." He is upset because he believes she said no to sun, romance, the blanket on the grass and getting to know him, when this was not the case at all — it was the ants, cold wet ground and shivering that she was rejecting! So there is one set of facts with two completely different interpretations. Make sure you always look at the facts objectively and don't inject a lot of misplaced meaning into them.

One phrase I have found to be incredibly helpful is: "What you mean by that, specifically?" This question will enable you to drill down to a certain level of detail so you can clearly understand the facts. Imagine if the girl in our picnic example had asked that question. The boy would have told her of his vision of sun, warmth and romance, and she would have been delighted. Together they would likely have figured out a wonderfully romantic date. Instead they are both upset and may never see each other again.

When you start getting upset about something, check your emotions at the door and ask yourself,

"Are these emotions helping me get to my end goal?" It's okay to have them, consult them and check in with them, but don't let them control you. Remember you are not your emotions and you do ultimately have complete control over them.

Emotions can also affect decision-making. One of the best pieces of advice I ever got was to always sleep on a decision before making it. It's also a good idea to avoid highly emotional discussions just before making a decision. Getting some distance allows your emotions to dissipate and for logic to surface.

✹ PICK YOUR BATTLES

One of the biggest drains on our time and energy is unnecessary interpersonal drama. Every one of us will occasionally be caught up in highly emotional situations that hijack all of our attention. Some of these are genuine crises requiring our response, but many are just not worth it. For example, how many times have you found yourself in a conversation in which you are certain you are right, and feel compelled to convince the other person of your point of view? You can spend a lot of time going back and forth, escalating the conversation to the point where it is a borderline argument, just to validate your point of view. Now I am all for standing up for what you believe in, but fighting tooth and nail to win every debate will drain your energy for no real gain, especially when the issue is just not that important. This kind of thing crops up all the time, both in personal situations and in business, so it is important to pick your battles carefully and only fight to win those that really matter.

You will not win every battle. In some cases you may find that your losses — mental, physical, spiritual or financial — are significant even if you win. If you allow yourself to be drawn into every power struggle and every minor debate, you can get caught in a whirlpool of negativity that will undermine your long-term goals by sucking up your energy.

Faced with opposition, disagreement or disapproval, ask yourself, "Is this really worth it?" "What do I really lose if I just walk away?" Being passionate about a cause or social injustice is one thing, but insisting on being right just for its own sake will never serve you in the long run. It's okay to assert an opinion and to share ideas with other people but it is not okay to try to push your ideas and beliefs onto other people, and trying to do so will usually backfire.

Be open to the thoughts and ideas of other people. There is a reason you have attracted these people into your life and you might find they have more to contribute than you think. Your approach has a great influence on the outcome of any exchange. If you can treat each person with kindness and respect, regardless of whether they are a beggar on the street or the CEO of a large company, you will find people will respect you more in return.

◉ TAKE CONTROL OF YOUR FINANCES

One of the fastest ways for a life to get derailed is through financial irresponsibility. I can't stress this strongly enough: To have a successful life, you must have a strong financial plan in place, and the financial responsibility to follow it. No matter your income level, it is critical that you know how much you have coming in and what your expenses are, and that you always stay ahead of the curve, not spending more than you make.

Create a spreadsheet with your monthly income across the top and your expenses listed below. Identify which expenses are absolutely necessary, like heat, groceries and electricity, and those that are not, such as manicures, a new car that comes with a larger car payment, or new clothes. If you find your expenses outweigh your income, cut back on non-essentials until your numbers add up. Try to set up a budget that allows you to put away a little bit — even just $20 — in a savings account every month. It sounds like a small amount, but the benefits are enormous. By making sure you always break even with at least some money to spare, not only will you be starting to save for your future, but you will also gain complete control of your expenses. Eventually you should strive to have at least eight months of living expenses in the bank to fall back on if you lose your job or face a major medical issue.

I know some people might say, "I can't even make ends meet, let alone save enough to go to college." But if you are determined to create a new life for yourself, you must have a "can do" attitude and find a way to make it happen.

Look at every area of your life to determine how you can invest more in yourself and waste less. If you think creatively, there is always something you can do to improve your financial position.

I once knew a woman who made $10 per hour. Her husband made $16 per hour and they had two kids. She was always dressed in somewhat expensive track-suits from labels like Juicy Couture. They ordered takeout every night for dinner and had two vehicles — a sports car and a GMC truck, both with hefty payments. On the outside everything looked great, but it was only a matter of time before they could not afford their car payments, fell behind on their rent and eventually got their cars seized by a repo man. They made a choice to put themselves in that situation. They were not responsible with their finances and made no effort to manage them. This would not have happened if they had lived within their means.

Often we see people who are struggling to make ends meet but somehow have the newest Xbox or PlayStation game consoles, or large TVs in their living rooms. By contrast, people who focus on creating wealth would rather put their money into a savings account or buy a bond or real estate, and sacrifice those material things that in a couple of years will have no value and eventually end up in the trash.

When I bought my first house at 18, I completely tapped out my modest savings, and the mortgage payments took my living expenses right to the edge of what I could afford. In fact, I had to cut back on some things. I could not afford to drive my car anymore, so I parked it and took the bus. I spent very little money on entertainment. I would go out with friends, but often would drink only water because I had no extra money for anything else. My focus was on my end goal of building some equity. One of my favorite sayings back then was "short-term pain for long-term gain." I knew that over time, my income would go up and eventually I would be able to afford more, but for the time being, I had to make those sacrifices. I also knew that in 25 years that house would be paid off and would be all mine.

As it turned out, I didn't end up owning that house for anything close to 25 years. My career took an upward turn when I got promoted to internal auditor. I had made some small improvements to the house, such as painting, which added to its charm. When I was 20, I sold that house for a profit of $14,000 — more money than I made in my job in a year. So all that cutting back and spending less paid off with big dividends. In fact, the inner discipline I developed by living within my means in that situation has paid off time and time again.

Spending less doesn't have to mean completely going without. When you are on a modest budget, thrift stores are great places to find nice suits and dresses that make you look professional and well put-together. If you look carefully, you can find great clothes in good condition — often, someone simply grew tired of them. In my life, I have known many people with money who still shop at thrift stores because they love to get a great deal. Also watch for the big sales. At certain times of the year, usually right before and after Christmas, I have snapped up beautiful suits for almost 70 percent off retail. If you stay within your budget and save your funds to get what you need when sales come around, you can still dress for success within your means. I certainly did that my first couple of years while working, always waiting for sales and buying only what I could afford.

One single thing that will make all the difference in your financial future is to pay off your credit card every month. Carrying a balance means you are paying the credit card companies 20 to 30 percent interest, if not more, on your spending. If you carry $1,000 on your card, you are paying the lender $200 a year for absolutely nothing. So make it a priority not to spend more than you have and to get those credit cards paid off every month.

If you have kids, consider setting up a babysitting co-op or share group. Band together with other parents to take turns once a week babysitting each other's kids. This will give all of you the break you need, plus time to focus on your future and building your skill set. You can do the same with house cleaning. Put together a group of three or four friends, then rotate from house to house to help each person clean every weekend. This transforms what would be a laborious and tiresome task into a fun and social experience. Besides, with three people cleaning and one person watching the kids, you will be able to get much more done in a shorter period of time.

You can apply the same strategy to maintaining a polished, professional look for yourself. Instead of paying for manicures or hair color, get together with a group of friends to have a glass of wine and do each other's hair or nails at regular manicure/pedicure parties.

On the flip side, if you have the means to bring in outside help, do it. Don't be afraid to hire house cleaners or babysitters to free up your time to study, exercise or do whatever you need to move yourself forward.

In the early years of my relationship with my husband, we both were working hard and I was starting to enjoy the benefits of my success. I was making a lot of money and working long hours. Invariably, by the time Saturday morning rolled around, our apartment was a mess; the kitchen and bathroom needed to be cleaned, the carpets vacuumed, and laundry done. We really needed to use our weekends for precious exercise and relaxation time, but instead we usually spent a few hours cleaning on Saturday mornings before we could go and enjoy ourselves. Over time I found this was wearing on me so I suggested we get a cleaning lady. My husband said he didn't think we needed one and that we each should do a little extra during the week. I knew that "little extra" would fall entirely on my shoulders. So I said, "Okay, you do a little extra each week and I am going to hire a cleaning lady to do my little extra." That put an end to that. I hired someone to come in for three hours on Friday. It felt so good to wake up to a clean and tidy apartment every Saturday; it completely freed my mind for the weekend.

The other important thing to note is that I took control of the situation. Even though I did not get the answer I wanted, I knew the burden would continue to fall more onto me than him, so I solved it. I was only able to do this because I was making enough money that I could afford to hire someone myself and was not relying on him for that. I had not allowed myself to become so financially dependent on a man that I lost control of my life.

Having control of your finances is one very important part of setting yourself up for success. If you are also able to control your emotions and create an environment that supports your success, you will be well on the way to creating your better life.

MAKE YOU YOUR TOP PRIORITY

"The difficulty lies not so much in developing new ideas as in escaping from old ones."

JOHN MAYNARD KEYNES

Despite the many legal strides women have made since the feminist movement of the 1960s and '70s, there is still an underlying assumption in our culture that women — especially those with children — should put the needs of everyone in their lives above their own. Their kids, their husband, their household, their extended family, friends, employer and just about anybody else who comes along is expected to get priority over the woman at the center of this web.

Ironically, the women who are most celebrated in our society — models, singers and actresses — are those who do make time for themselves, ensuring they get enough exercise, rest and proper nutrition to stay fit and beautiful. So why do we feel guilty and face the judgment of others if we tend to our own well-being? Often we are our own harshest critics in this area, perpetuating the stigma by branding our self-nurturing attempts as "selfish."

Nurturing, generosity and caregiving are wonderful things. But all good things can turn negative when they are out of balance. Consistently focusing on the needs of others can lead us to neglect our own health and well-being, and deny ourselves the things that bring us pleasure. If you are always looking after others while running yourself dry, it will wear on you over time, resulting in frustration, unhappiness and lower self-esteem without you even realizing what has happened. Worse, it will hold you back from your pursuit of a better life.

Our culture tends to support men spending time with other men, pursuing their careers and fulfilling themselves mentally, but we do not necessarily put the same value on women's care and fulfillment. In the face of this cultural bias, I think women especially should make deliberate efforts to take care of themselves mentally, physically and emotionally. Whatever your long-term plan for your life, it is important to take time to exercise, have social time with friends and to think and connect with yourself.

Of course, men can and do fall into the same patterns of self-neglect, whether it is because they are focusing all their efforts on taking care of their family or simply because they have developed poor habits.

Both men and women on ambitious career tracks tend to short-change themselves, neglecting their physical and emotional health while pouring all their energy into reaching their goals. Over time, those unhealthy lifestyle habits can cause lasting damage and become stubbornly resistant to change. I believe that in order to thrive as a healthy and functional society, we need to place a higher value on ourselves and make our well-being a priority. This starts with each of us caring for ourselves as the precious, beautiful beings that we truly are.

If you're raising children you may find this very challenging. Even if you have set yourself up for success as we talked about in the last chapter, you might feel torn between your children's needs and yours, worrying that it would appear selfish to hire a babysitter just so you could go to the gym. If you are a single parent on a low income, it's especially hard to justify using your precious limited resources on time for yourself. But if you are a single parent, it's even more important — for your kids as well as for yourself — that you set goals that will bring you all a better life, and that you give yourself the nurturing you need in order to reach them. You are all your children have. As their provider and their role model, you need to make sure you are going to be around for them as long as possible, and that you show up every day excited about life and feeling good about yourself. All of these elements will affect the kind of parent you are to your children. What better investment in your family can you make than investing in its leader?

Women often feel they should be able to do it all on their own, but it is okay to ask for help, and a strong, confident woman knows when she needs it. If there are areas of your life where you need a hand, don't be afraid to ask for it. If people who you know and trust offer to help, say yes! If money is truly tight and free family support is not available, try asking for help at your church or within your religious community. Let them know you are working to get ahead and that you need some support in your home; you may need a few hours of babysitting and house cleaning each day. There are many grandmothers with time on their hands and caretaking skills who would love to restore a sense of purpose to their daily routine. You won't find them if you don't ask. Accept that help and use it to build yourself up, because the road to success requires mental strength, emotional stability and physical stamina.

◉ EMOTIONAL WELL-BEING

When I reflect back on my biggest challenges and missed opportunities, I can see they all stemmed from not taking care of myself emotionally. I had come from a childhood environment of such neglect that it bordered on abandonment.

I will never forget the moment when I realized just how much I would have to fend for myself in life. I was seven years old, sitting at the kitchen table ready to do my second grade spelling homework. My mom sat with me, staring blankly at the words on the page. I remember asking her several times with growing impatience, "Mom, can you tell me what these words are?"

She just stared at the worksheet and tilted her head. "Mommy doesn't know those words."

I didn't understand. "Don't all mommies know these words?" I asked.

"Mommy doesn't know those words. I'm sorry honey, but I'm not as smart as you are," she said as she turned her attention back to the soap opera on TV.

I sat there in shock. I had already noticed my mother was a slow reader and there were some words she did not know. But in that moment I realized that at seven years old, my reading level had surpassed hers. This didn't make me feel proud or pleased with myself. It made me feel very alone. I knew then that I had only myself to rely on.

Neglect and abuse often runs in families, passed down from one generation to the next through ignorance, poor role modeling and learned behavior. My mother's father was an alcoholic who left his wife to raise their six young children alone. Bitter and unable to cope, my grandmother neglected and physically abused my mother and her siblings, leaving my mom with no access to supportive adults who might have helped her grow and develop despite her limited intellectual capacity. I later learned she was educated in a strict Catholic school — which at the time was not a good place for a left-handed child. Every time she used that hand to pick up a pencil, the nuns would slap it with a ruler. Between that mistreatment and her learning disabilities, it's no surprise she failed second grade three times and shut herself off completely from any new learning.

That night I cried myself to sleep, as I had done many times. But this time was different. I buried my head in my pillow and quietly sobbed. "My mom can't read, my dad is never around, and there's no one else to help me. There is no one to help me," I whispered to myself. I had never felt so alone.

The insecurity that came from this upbringing was the very reason that I did not accept the card from the L'Oreal representative who suggested I might become a cosmetics model. In other situations, my anxiety has caused me to come on too strong, damaging or even ruining relationships. I have missed out on what might have been some of the biggest opportunities of my life because I hadn't healed emotionally from the wounds of the past.

If you encountered abuse, neglect or other forms of trauma as a child, I can tell you that your "normal" is not everyone's normal. For me, it was like having a constant weight on my chest that I ignored for a very long time until I was finally ready to deal with it. I also struggled with a constant sense of loneliness that I just could not shake. But it wasn't until after I had my children and my mother passed away that these issues became pressing for me.

In my interactions with my children, I sometimes felt I was acting out negative old family patterns, and worried that my past could be affecting my kids. My past wasn't all negative — I learned some things that make me a good mother — but when I watched how other mothers parented, I began to see I could do better at nurturing. Finally I went to a therapist and did a one-on-one counseling program called Lifespan Integration Therapy, for people who have suffered neglect and trauma. It helped heal many of my old wounds. Together the therapist and I essentially reprogrammed the parts of my brain that held deep, old, extremely painful memories by reimagining those distressing events with new, more positive and nurturing details. I dreaded going to our sessions because I knew how painful it would be to relive some of these old memories, but within a few days of each session, I noticed my feelings of loneliness and anxiety would dissipate.

Now that I have processed some of this old pain, my only regret is that I didn't do it sooner because I can see how much more power I have without those issues holding me back.

Healing can take place in many ways. Reading self-help books is a great place to start. There are also many seminars and courses that can help you process the past. Those of us who have gone through extreme situations either in childhood or adulthood may need the intensive treatment of one-on-one therapy. I was able to function well in my life and achieve great success, but I still carried a deep sense of loneliness and anxiety that could only be healed through professional counseling.

Journaling can also be an effective tool. It's important to let yourself feel your emotions, and writing them down on paper can help you process them. When I have a disappointment or a loss, I write down how I feel and why I feel that way. It gives me a way to process and then release those emotions.

If you are struggling with deep-rooted pain that is with you every day; if you constantly feel alone or have anxious thoughts that you are not good enough, or emotional pain that frequently has you in tears, you need professional help. If finances are an issue, resources may be available. If you live in Canada, your family doctor should be able to make a referral to an outpatient mental health program. If you are in the US without a healthcare plan that covers mental health treatment, try calling private therapists to ask if they do pro-bono work, or whether they offer a sliding scale of fees. Some private practitioners reserve a certain number of hours per week to help those who can't afford their full rates. Whatever your situation, don't be afraid to do some research and advocate for yourself. Consider this one of the most significant gifts you can give yourself. It goes to the foundation of who you are, and will give you the ability to experience more confidence and joy than you thought possible.

Even if you're not burdened with the aftermath of traumatic events, it's important to take care of yourself emotionally; to always be aware of your circumstances and how they affect you, and not to stay in situations that deplete you. To do this, you have to give yourself permission to process your feelings as they come up, without suppressing them or being consumed by them.

One aspect of emotional health that we can all practice is forgiveness. It's easy to carry a grudge when another person has harmed us, whether physically, mentally, emotionally or financially. But allowing that anger to percolate in our hearts only hurts us. Forgiveness is one of the kindest things we can do for ourselves. If someone has wronged you, forgiving them does not mean you are saying their behavior is okay. Rather, you are letting go of the anger so you can open your heart completely to let love and kindness in. So take a few minutes to consider whether you are holding any grudges, then make a conscious effort to forgive and let them go. Write them down if you need to. Once you have forgiven, you will feel a sense of calm pass through your body, freeing you up to attract more positive energy into your life.

Each of us will have our share of disappointments and heartache in our lives. No matter who you are, there will be times when you will be upset about a particular situation, but you don't have to allow your emotions to stop you in your tracks. Acknowledge your feelings by saying to yourself, "Okay, I am upset right now." You might even need to have a good cry. Then take those emotions and put them off to one side. Don't suppress them, but don't let them control you or divert you from your path, either. Stay focused on your end goal. It might help to tell yourself, "I acknowledge that I have these feelings, but I actively choose to make decisions that will continue to move me forward, and not make decisions based on these emotions." This is a critically important practice if you are to keep moving forward and not be thwarted by your emotions.

☀ PHYSICAL WELL-BEING

Your body is your vehicle for moving through life, and its well-being has a direct impact on your journey. If you're always exhausted and lacking nutrients or exercise, it's difficult to show up every day to take on the challenges that await you.

Sleep is one of the most important yet most widely neglected aspects of good physical health. You might think an early bedtime is just for kids, or that being ambitious and successful means burning the candle at both ends. Nothing could be further from the truth. Yes, there are super-human people who seem to do fine on four to six hours of sleep per night, but most of us need seven to eight and a half hours every night in order to function well.

Notice whether you regularly wake up tired, or if you hit the snooze button so often that you're already late by the time you get out of bed. Ask yourself: Is this really the tone I want to set for my day? Is this the behavior of an in-control person who is creating a new and better life? Or is this a person who gives in to the temptations of late-night TV and undisciplined habits? A seemingly small but consistently repeated decision can become a defining moment.

The choice you make between turning in for the night and wasting another hour on trivial entertainment or social media can have a huge impact not only on your energy the next morning but on the overall trajectory of your life. Is it worth sacrificing your sleep — and consequently not having the energy you need to achieve what you want — just to watch Jimmy Fallon's monologue? Or are you prepared to push out of your comfort zone and step into a more disciplined arena?

You may have a hard time getting to bed at a decent hour simply because you have too much to do once you get home from work. I hear this a lot from working mothers, with their heavy job- and family-related workloads.

Schedules, routines and clear priorities are the saving grace for those of us with a lot of responsibilities on our plate. Ask yourself: What are the most important things you need to focus on when you get home? Spending time with your children, feeding them a nutritious dinner and helping them with their homework are obviously top priorities.

To allow enough time for these important things, think about what you can do differently to ease the rest of your workload. Are your children old enough to start helping with light chores? Do they have a schedule telling them exactly what is expected of them and when? My eight-year-old twins know they are responsible for unloading the dishwasher and helping set the table. My ten-year-old daughter knows she has to put away any pots that are washed and drying on the counter, and also helps with some light cooking. If your kids know, for example, that 6–7 pm is for homework and nothing else, you will cut out a lot of time that might have been spent arguing. When preparing dinner, try making enough for two or three meals and freezing some so you can pull dinner out of the freezer and put it in the microwave on days when you're short of time. Systems like these can help minimize your household burden and give you more time to unwind and rest properly at the end of the day.

Finally, examine the quality of your sleep. Millions of North Americans suffer from various types of sleep issues, ranging from difficulty falling asleep to repeated midnight waking. If you are one of those, get yourself to a doctor to find a solution. If your family doctor brushes it off, find another who will work with you until you solve the problem. For years, I suffered from not being able to fall asleep even when I was exhausted. Finally I went to a sleep doctor who in one visit gave me a variety of helpful tools and tips so that now most nights I am able to fall asleep without much trouble. I have also learned that I am so sensitive to caffeine that I can't have any type of it after 2 pm, or my sleep will be disrupted. Even a small bite of brownie or piece of chocolate will keep me up. Getting to know your body and accepting its particular limits will help you to support yourself in the way you need.

◉ DIET AND EXERCISE

Most of us lead pretty sedentary lives. Without regular exercise, our bodies just don't get physically tired enough to rest well at night. We also find ourselves carrying around too much stress with no release for it. Exercise is not only great for the body; it is great for the mind too.

In the early years of my career I found that although I was doing well, I often felt stressed and sometimes overwhelmed. I found a good workout made me feel strong and in control, clearing my mind and rejuvenating my body.

I'm not an expert in diet and exercise, and it's beyond the scope of this book to offer specific advice in those areas. But I have learned through experience the difference that healthy habits can make, and what can go wrong when we don't practice them.

When I was 18 years old and modeling, I was obsessed with being thin. That and the fact that I had very little money for food led me to drastically under-feed myself. At the time I didn't understand my body. I was at a healthy weight for my height but not a desir-able model weight. Although I ate very little, I could not seem to get as thin as I wanted. Sometimes, a bran muffin or a bowl of soup would hold me for an entire day. But then would come days of intense cravings, when I would stuff myself with potato chips or other junk food. I'd follow this up with a round of laxatives, hoping they would send the food through me without weight gain. What I didn't know was that by starving my body and not exercising regularly, I was losing muscle mass and slowing down my metabolism.

Years later as a busy mother of three young chil-dren in my early 40s, I began taking shortcuts on my health, giving in to cravings and snacking on foods that did not give my body the nutrients it needed. I ended up carrying a few extra pounds I just could not lose. After some experimentation, I found my body responded best to a diet high in vegetables with at least three servings of protein each day. I also replaced processed snacks with nuts and vegetables. Once I figured out the optimal diet for my body, I found I could eat enough food to satisfy me every day and still maintain a healthy weight. My energy and overall sense of well-being improved too.

✸ MENTAL WELL-BEING

We've talked a lot about clearing your mind of negative thoughts, but that's only one side of mental well-being. It's also critical to make time for your imagination so you can tap into your creative side and expand your ideas. Try to do at least one thing every day that brings you joy and stimulates your intellect. Allowing yourself space to explore your interests exercises the mind and adds richness to your life. Are you fascinated by art or music? Endlessly interested in Ancient Rome, organic gardening, Japanese culture or ornithology? Study it. Give yourself permission to read, research and immerse yourself in it. Diving deep into your passions may even lead to new business ideas or career opportunities, as you become an expert in what was once just a hobby.

You also need regular, undistracted time to think strategically about your life. This is time to prepare for possible obstacles or opportunities that may be on the horizon. As new situations arise or existing ones change, this advance thinking will enable you to calmly develop clear, well-thought-out plans for action, rather than feeling blindsided and unprepared.

One critical factor that affects our entire being is stress. We all have stress in our lives, from our jobs, personal relationships and lifestyle habits. Allowing it to get out of hand by not addressing its root cause will strain us emotionally, physically and mentally. It works the other way around too — unhealthy mental, physical and emotional habits will increase stress levels, leading to a vicious cycle that can be hard to break.

See if you can identify which areas of your life cause you the most stress, and try to understand why that is. If you are overwhelmed by your responsibilities, take another look at your support system, and how you might be able to call in some extra help to reduce tension and anxiety. If your stress stems from a lack of direction and purpose, go back to creating your future from the future — getting a solid plan in place to meet your goals will alleviate some of that stress. Are there people in your life who make you feel down and emotional? Look at how to lessen their impact on your life and how you might add new relationships with people who believe in you, including mentors, coaches and guides. Taking stock of your own personal sources of stress will give you significant insights into the parts of your life that you might want to focus on first as you work toward creating a better life.

◉ THE OUTSIDE IS A REFLECTION OF THE INSIDE

Your physical presentation is important in so many ways. If you want to be successful in life, paying attention to your appearance is a practical necessity that has nothing to do with vanity. We all judge each other all the time based on our looks and how we carry ourselves. In any context, this is simply about looking well-maintained and appropriate for the situation.

When you don't put your best foot forward in terms of your appearance, you are sending a message that you don't feel so good about yourself, that your standards are low, or maybe even that you are too lazy to put any effort into yourself. Treating your looks with care, ensuring that you are well-groomed and dressed appropriately, signals confidence, self-respect and good judgment.

You're allowed to be laid back and lazy when you're at home sick, but how about when you're out shopping, or socializing with friends? You never know who is watching or whom you might run into. If you're always looking good, you'll attract more opportunities, and you'll feel ready to handle them when they arise, no matter how unexpected.

Of course, your personal presentation at work is crucial. When you show up at your job every day, what do your coworkers or customers see? Are you looking your absolute best, well put-together self or are you looking haphazard? Your appearance is vital because it's all part of the message you send to the external world, and shapes all your interactions with it.

Remember that you are building your own personal brand. What image do you want your brand to project? If you work in a professional or corporate setting, a nice suit will do wonders to elevate your image, even if it's not strictly necessary in your current role. Dressing for the job you want to grow into will help your bosses see you in that light and can make a difference when promotions are being handed out. If on the other hand you work in an informal setting, jeans and a nice top might be more appropriate, but make sure they are clean and sized right for your body.

Whatever your style and workplace setting, good maintenance is key. This means not wearing clothes that are ill-fitting, or even slightly stained or torn. If you prefer long painted nails but can't afford to keep them up, wear them short with no polish. That is a much nicer, more professional look than walking around with broken nails and chipped nail polish. If you don't have the means to keep things up, it's better to go for a simple, clean look that you can maintain.

You don't need to spend beyond your means to keep yourself looking polished and presentable. Instead of going to a fancy salon that charges $200 for a haircut, try discount hairdressers such as Supercuts, which can do a perfectly good haircut for very little money, especially if you go for a simple style. Another money-saving option is to go to hairdressing schools, where students under instructors' supervision offer haircuts and color for free or for a very low fee. A new suit could set you back hundreds of dollars, but if you spend a little time exploring thrift stores, you can always find a nice slightly used one for next to nothing. If you have a little more money to spend, bargain stores like T.J. Maxx or Winners are great options where you can usually pick up a few nice pieces for less than a hundred dollars.

Don't fall into the trap of thinking you are "investing" in your shoes or clothes. Everything wears out and goes out of style eventually, and a wardrobe of modestly priced clothing that is replaced and updated often will make a better impression than designer clothes that are on their way to looking shabby or no longer fit your body type.

❂ TAKE CARE OF YOUR SPACE

Early on in my marriage, I had a dedicated workspace in our home. But instead of feeling productive and happy in it, I found that every time I sat there to work I quickly became frustrated and distracted.

It took me a while to figure out the problem. I found that my husband was constantly dumping all the excess mail and household paperwork on my desk, and it was the regular unexpected mess that was frustrating me. I now know that when my office is a mess, it paralyzes me, and I cannot get work done.

I asked my husband several times to stop using my desk as a dumping ground. At first it didn't register and he continued to do it, until I finally became angry with him for not respecting me or my space. It got to the point where I asked that he keep away from my workspace completely. Whenever I found a mess on my desk, I simply moved it back to where it came from. It took a while, but he finally understood the impact it was having on me.

Now whenever my own clutter starts piling up, I simply remove everything from my desk, put it on the floor and go through it one item at a time, dealing with it, filing it, or throwing it away. This method of dealing with clutter can be applied to other chores and demands — just deal with each thing methodically, one at a time, until the pile is gone.

Each of us has our blind spots when it comes to health and wellness. You might be great at keeping an orderly environment but have a tendency to neglect your diet. Or you might be in peak physical condition but struggling to shift some old emotional baggage. We all have areas in which we could do better, and working on those issues is a lifelong process, so don't demand perfection of yourself. There's nothing healthy about harsh criticism and self-judgment! Nurturing yourself calls for tenderness, patience, and appreciation

of your own unique personality, flaws and all. Regardless of your weaknesses, loving and accepting yourself
just as you are even as you strive to do better may be the
very best thing you can do for your own well-being.

MAGNIFY YOUR EXISTENCE

"Be thankful for what you have; you'll end up having more. If you concentrate on what you don't have, you will never, ever have enough."

OPRAH WINFREY

There is no greater gift you can give yourself than the act of giving to another person. It's a beautiful and fundamental law of life that when you are generous with yourself and your resources, you will in turn attract more generosity into your life. When you truly embrace generosity as a way of being, more opportunities to receive all the good that life has to offer will present themselves to you, and you will feel more open to receiving them.

Generosity is closely related to abundance — the energy of wealth. By making yourself an opening through which generosity flows, you will also keep the energy of abundance flowing through your life. As you begin to achieve your goals and see your new life take shape, your financial picture will improve. This will not only will fuel your personal fulfillment, your health, and your family's well-being, but also create an opportunity to make a positive impact on the world and the lives of people you touch. Supporting causes you believe in, helping individuals in need, and investing in the success of those who follow in your footsteps all bring deep meaning to your own success.

But generosity goes beyond money; it covers all aspects of life. The philanthropic community refers to time, treasure and talent as the three big ways in which people give back. This means sharing your efforts, financial resources or skills. And you don't need to wait for wealth before you start making a difference. The sooner you begin to practice the life-affirming attitude of generosity, the greater positive energy and goodwill you will attract as you continue your journey.

Walking down the street, you may notice someone struggling with a package, or an elderly person having trouble crossing the street. Offer to help — you have no idea how much a small random act of kindness can affect another person's life. Perhaps you are on the subway and you see someone who looks distressed. Give the person your seat, and notice the difference it makes in how you feel. In our busy, mobile-device-focused, driven culture, it's easy to become so self-focused that we forget how to be generous in our everyday lives. Especially in the early phase of striving toward our goals, we can get caught in "me-first" thinking. But when we take the time to extend ourselves to our fellow human beings, we are demonstrating to ourselves that the world can be a friendly place filled with supportive allies. Try it, and notice the feeling of gratitude that comes from knowing that you live in such a world.

◉ GENEROSITY AND GRATITUDE GO HAND IN HAND

Remind yourself every day of everything you are grateful for. This will not only draw more of these gifts toward you, but help you appreciate them more when they come. If you focus on what you don't have, you will be miserable and frustrated, and even worse, miss out on the good things you do have. Such an attitude is almost like throwing a gift back in the giver's face without ever benefiting or deriving any happiness from it. Instead of focusing on what you don't have, use affirmations such as "I'm thankful for my home" or "I'm thankful for my family" to boost your appreciation. You might even find it helpful to write these statements in a gratitude journal. Every evening, take a few minutes to list the things in your life for which you are grateful. This is a great exercise to do before bed because it puts you in a calm and peaceful state in preparation for sleep.

Once you're in the habit of counting your blessings, the next step is to be thankful for what is yet to come. Being grateful for the wonderful things, people and events that are just around the corner allows you to align your goals, plans and visions with the very future you want to create. These can go into your gratitude journal too, making your future accomplishments more real and concrete in your mind and drawing you closer to realizing them.

When you truly open your heart in this way, you tap into a source of love that is always within you, and you will attract more of the actions and experiences that create that love. Use that power to revive and enrich yourself; use it to find your true nature and your true path. When you love yourself unconditionally and permit yourself to feel love for everything around you, your life will reflect that love back to you, and be rich with experience.

When we appreciate what we have, we naturally want to extend that good feeling of plenty to others by sharing. That starts a virtuous circle, because sharing makes us feel rich in our resources, and therefore even more grateful. Each quality tends to increase the other.

Performing even the smallest act of kindness makes you feel different inside. Even your appearance is affected. The lines on your face will soften and your eyes will exude contentment and happiness. This look is naturally attractive to others. By contrast, no one is drawn to people who look angry; in fact, most of us run from them. So think about how you are coming across every day: Do you appear kind and generous or selfish and stingy? None of us lives in a bubble, so every exchange we have affects the way people respond to us.

You can bring this full circle — by acknowledging the people around you for what makes them wonderful. Single out at least one aspect of each person in your life for a compliment. For example: "I just want to acknowledge you for being a great friend. You are always there for me and I really appreciate it." Allow the compliment to land and notice the effect it has on the person. Do this from an authentic place, for the pure joy of giving another person a boost, and not with the expectation of getting a compliment back in return. Too often, we take a transactional approach to compliments, and they come across as self-interested, obligatory or insincere. If compliments come with strings attached, they tend to bring the other person down instead of building them up.

One day when my twin girls were around five years old, I took them to do some banking with me. Out of the blue, one of my girls said to the bank teller, "I like your nails." And that was it; short, sweet and sincere. That bank teller's face lit up with biggest smile as she looked at my daughter and said, "Thank you!" It would never have even occurred to me to compliment her on her nails, which were very long, very blue and very shiny. But coming from my daughter, that compliment was authentic, and I could see that it shifted that teller's entire state of being in that moment.

There are so many ways to give that can make significant differences in the lives of many people without it ever feeling like work. When you approach life from a place of kindness and generosity, it is easy to be there for other people.

As you move along the path to success, you will encounter people who remind you of an earlier version of yourself. Some may even be in the same place you started from. When this happens, as it inevitably does to all successful people, I encourage you to reach out and be a mentor or guide to them, in the same way others may be mentoring you now. Validation and encouragement from someone who has been there and overcome some of the same challenges could be all that's required for a person to open up to a whole new potential in his or herself.

Even one conversation can alter the path of someone's life. I'm thinking about a woman I met during a business trip to Orlando, Florida who intrigued me over a quick drink she had with me and the mutual friend who introduced us. The woman's English was poor and she struggled to express her thoughts and feelings. It became clear to me she had a strong desire to do more with her life but didn't know how to go about it.

I had no plans for the following evening so I gave her my number and offered to meet her to talk about her situation if she was interested. I didn't expect her to take me up on it, but when she called, I figured that since she was bold enough to take that step, I would certainly meet her.

At our meeting, I learned that she was 37, had come to the United States from Paraguay 20 years earlier, and had spent all that time working as a cleaning lady and kitchen help at a hotel. Despite her decades in the us, she had very few friends in the community, and even had some people in her social circle who insulted her and brought her down. Her goals were to get married one day and to open her own cleaning business. She asked me what I thought she should do.

Here was this woman who had come from a very poor situation in Paraguay as a girl and had spent all those years working laborious jobs in America to help support her family back home. All of this was very admirable, except for one thing: she had not taken care of herself and she had neglected to build her skills along the way. Even after so long in the us, her English was choppy and at times hard to understand.

Moved by her determination and passion, I told her she was beautiful and smart, and advised her to take an English course to boost her confidence and ability to communicate, as well as a business course if she was planning to open a business with employees. These courses would also be a great way to meet people who were motivated just like her, I told her. Finally, I encouraged her to always try to look her best, and not to spend time with people who made her feel bad about herself.

After a very nice evening I went home, knowing I would probably never see this woman again and unsure about what she would do with my words of encouragement. I followed up in the morning with an email summarizing my advice and wishing her all the best.

The very next day she replied. She said she had already enrolled in an English class and was planning to enroll in a business class. She expressed deep gratitude, saying she wanted to be a successful woman just like me, and that I would be very proud of her in a few years.

I am not suggesting you have dinner with every stranger you meet, but the encounter was a reminder of how just one conversation can potentially alter the course of another person's life for the better. Every time I read her email, it brings me joy and comfort. It's a reminder to me of what's really important.

⦿ APPLY GOOD SENSE TO YOUR GIVING

When you achieve success, you will find calls for help coming at you from all directions. One of the best things about affluence is that it gives you the power to help in ways that are meaningful to you, or ways in which you feel your support is most urgently needed or can make the biggest difference. It's your right to choose where you will concentrate your giving, based on your own personal values. As much as we might like to solve all the world's problems, there is nothing wrong with being selective, and this means saying no to some requests.

Be smart and purposeful about your gifts and contributions. There are many causes and individuals needing a lot of time and money, and it is important to respect your personal boundaries with regard to this. We have all heard stories about people who have given all their money to some cause they believe in. That may seem like the ultimate in generosity, but it is not necessarily so if it depletes your capacity to care for yourself and your own family, who are your number one responsibility. So be generous of spirit, but wise with your pocketbook and time. You can still be supportive to those who matter most to you while maintaining your boundaries and taking care of what you need to.

With money comes a certain level of responsibility. Handle it with discipline, respect and make plans for how it will meet your future needs. Being wasteful and frivolous is not the same as being generous. Ostentatious displays of wealth, such as taking all your friends on holidays you can't really afford, might actually indicate you are more caught up in materialism and status symbols than planning a secure future for yourself and your family. Respect the work that went into earning your money, and avoid excessive spending on things that will not maintain their value over time.

As rewarding as it is to give back, it doesn't mean you have to give *it* back. If you are a kind-hearted and generous person who loves to give, you will have no shortage of opportunities to do so, but stay within the capacity of your resources. As with spending, it is possible for giving to get out of control and deplete you, especially when the recipients have a direct line to your heart.

During the summer of 2003 when I was six months' pregnant with my first daughter, I got a phone call. "Give me $60,000 or I will kill myself," said the caller.

I recognized the voice immediately as that of a relative. This person had racked up credit card debt of $60,000 and had no money to pay the bill. Despite being on a disability pension, this person had developed extravagant spending habits, purchasing many unnecessary things such as two vehicles, two cell phones and a custom built computer. Ironically, some of these items were things I did not even have myself.

At first, I was speechless and terrified that the threat would be carried out. But when I listened to my gut, I knew that handing over the money would not solve the person's problems.

I urged my relative to seek help from a psychiatrist for the suicidal thoughts and from a credit counselor for the money problems. The response? "Just let me know if you won't give me the money, because I have a few things to take care of before I kill myself."

I was shaken and intimidated, especially when this person manipulated other family members to pressure me to give in. I knew I was being targeted because I had money, which I would gladly have given if it would have solved the problem. Struggling with what to do, I talked to professionals in the medical world, whose advice was always the same: This person had to deal with this on their own, and find a way to be able to live within their means.

When I got a phone call echoing the same threat a few days later, I finally called the police and my relative was taken in for a psychiatric evaluation. I never learned the exact diagnosis, but the attending psychiatrist later told me that giving in would certainly have been a mistake, and would likely have only led to more and more demands for money in the years to come. Paying off the credit card debt would not have been a charitable act. In fact, it would have had the opposite effect because I would have been enabling and encouraging the unrealistic spending habits that caused the trouble to start with.

Being generous does not mean being an enabler or a pushover, and it does not mean allowing yourself to be bullied. Don't be afraid to stand your ground if you find people coming to you for money with strong-arm tactics, or if they resent you for your success.

If you are one of the fortunate few who earns more than enough money to live comfortably, you are in the joyful position of being able to make a real difference in people's lives. The whole point of success in life is to share it with others because you can't take it with you, and eventually, we are remembered by the difference we make in the world.

You don't have to wait until you are incredibly successful to give back; sometimes we can learn as much from people who are just a few steps ahead of us as we can from people who have reached the pinnacle of success. It is never too soon to share your insight and encouragement. Even while you are journeying toward your better life, at any point along the way you can be an inspiration for someone else.

When I was 23 years old, I was asked to speak to a group of girls at an inner city high school about what it takes to be a successful woman. I was still modeling at the time, doing fashion shows and photo shoots. I had also sold my first house and bought a couple more, and had finished my CMA designation, so although I really was not that much older than they were, I had some life experience they could learn from.

During my speech, I was struck by how hungry these girls were for guidance and information. I gave a message of inspiration, telling them they could do anything they put their minds to. Later I spent some time teaching them how to walk like a model and how to carry themselves. I had every single girl get up and walk. As they laughed nervously and good-naturedly teased each other I could see myself in them, remembering the first time I walked on the ramp at the modeling school. I had been petrified, but I had pushed myself to do it, and that experience gave me a certain courage that I wanted to pass along to anyone struggling with doubt about their potential.

Giving back to that classroom of girls is to this day one of my fondest memories. The joy and excitement in their eyes was the greatest gift anyone could have given me, planting a seed that has grown into this book, and continues to find new avenues of expression in my personal, professional and philanthropic life.

The beauty of this journey is that it never ends. Success is not a fixed destination, after which life stops bringing you challenges and opportunities. You just keep going deeper and deeper into your own potential.

The lessons I learned on my road from rags to riches are the very same lessons I learn again and again each day. The goals I set for myself now may be very different from the ones I set for myself as I was leaving Garson at the age of 17, but the principles remain unchanged.

I still use affirmations to remind myself to believe in myself when I encounter doubt and fear. (That's right — it does still happen.) Doubt and fear are an unavoidable part of life, and I have learned the secret to reducing their negative influence is managing them rather than trying to eliminate them.

I still draw upon my dreams when setting goals and making plans for the future. The vision keeps changing and expanding, so there is always a new horizon to conquer. Once I've settled on a new goal, I still plan meticulously when working toward it. At this point in my life, planning is second nature. In fact, I trust this process so much that I start getting excited about my goals coming to fruition as soon a plan is in place. And they almost always do!

I still seek to surround myself with people who believe in me, and who inspire me to be the best friend or family member I can possibly be. These people all add to my continually developing support system for success. After mentoring many others in my life, I am always on the lookout for mentors, sponsors and inspirational figures of my own — and I delight in the many ways they show up in my life.

I still take care of myself inside and out. After all, this body, mind and heart have taken me this far, so why wouldn't I treat them with love and respect?

And of course, more than ever, I still love to give back.

It is my sincere wish that the lessons contained in this book can serve as a beacon for you as you travel your own road to success. Whether you dream of running a Fortune 500 company or simply getting out of debt and putting your kids through college, I know without a doubt that the better life that lives within your heart is also within your reach.

ACKNOWLEDGMENTS

It takes a village to write a book, and I would like to acknowledge the following people for their extra efforts throughout this process: My daughters, for their patience during the many hours I spent poring over the computer; my countless friends, who gave me support and encouragement, especially when I doubted myself; Maggie Langrick, for hanging in there through thick and thin; Vince Poscente and Peter Thomas, for inspiring me to write this book; Bill Auger, for being a true friend and mentor; and Malcolm Parry, for supporting my vision from the very beginning.